Brother Animal

". . . from the very beginning I realized it was this very struggle in Tausk that most deeply moved me—the struggle of the human creature. Brother-animal. You."

LOU ANDREAS-SALOMÉ
The Freud Journal

BROTHER ANIMAL

The Story of Freud and Tausk

by Paul Roazen

VINTAGE BOOKS
A Division of Random House / New York

Contents

INTRODUCTION

How I Came Upon This Story

*I*n the fall of 1964 I started to meet and interview everyone living who had ever known Sigmund Freud. It was at first something of a fishing expedition, as I had little assurance that I would be successful in finding these people or that, once found, they would be willing to speak with me. And if they did, could I learn very much that was not already in history books?

So I began tentatively—though spurred on by no idle curiosity. For I had already spent several years in the company of Freud's ideas while preparing a manuscript on the moral and political implications of his work (subsequently revised and published as *Freud: Political and Social Thought*).* Thus I was naturally intrigued by the idea of meeting some of those who had helped shape the intellectual life of our century. As I sought them out, how-

* (New York: Alfred A. Knopf; 1968)

ever, I was amazed to learn how much more they could reveal about the history and personalities of Freud's circle than the books through which that early era had been known to me. By seeing more and more of Freud's pupils, relatives, and enemies—he was known to them all simply as "Professor"—I found that the great man began for the first time to live in my mind as a human being.

If I had any explicit aim at the outset, it was to gather the oral tradition of Freud's circle. For what seems gossip to one generation may be history to the next. All these people were elderly, and every year fewer of them will be alive. It took about three years of interviewing, including several trips to Europe and much travel around America, to complete my study. My way led from Park Avenue offices in New York to Harley Street consulting rooms in London; from a palace in Switzerland to a villa in the mountains outside Mexico City; and of course from the London house where Freud died—now something of a latter-day shrine—to the Viennese apartment in which for so many years he lived, now partially transformed into a seamstress's shop.

In the end I succeeded in talking with over seventy people who had known Freud, in addition to another thirty or so who had participated in the early days of psychoanalysis. My work snowballed, one person leading to others, until I had met twenty-five of Freud's analytic patients, as well as three of his children, his sister-in-law, two daughters-in-law, and several nieces and nephews. At the time of this writing over a dozen of these people have already passed away.

Here is a partial list of the people who were good enough to help me with their time and hospitality:

Mrs. Karl Abraham, Dr. Alexandra Adler, Dr. Michael Balint, Dr. Therese Benedek, Dr. E. A. Bennet, Sir Isaiah Berlin, Mr. Edward Bernays, Miss Hella Bernays, Dr. Bruno Bettelheim, Dr. Smiley Blanton, Miss Berta Bornstein, Dr. John Bowlby, Dr. David Brunswick, Prof. Mark Brunswick, Dr. Helene Deutsch, Dr. Kurt Eissler, Prof. & Mrs. Erik Erikson, Mr. Ernst Federn, Dr. Michael Fordham, Dr. Thomas French, Mrs. Alexander Freud, Miss Anna Freud, Dr. Esti Freud, Mr. & Mrs. Oliver Freud, Dr. Erich Fromm, Dr. William Gillespie, Dr. Edward Glover, Mr. Geoffrey Gorer, Dr. Roy Grinker, Sr., Dr. Martin Grotjahn, Dr. Heinz Hartmann, Dr. Paula Heimann, Mrs. Judith Bernays Heller, Dr. Ives Hendrick, Mr. Albert Hirst, Mrs. Edward Hitschmann, Dr. Willi Hoffer, Dr. Richard Hoffmann, Mrs. Mathilda Freud Hollitscher, Dr. Otto Isakower, Dr. Edith Jackson, Dr. Jolandi Jacobi, Dr. Robert Jokl, Mrs. Ernest Jones, Dr. Abram Kardiner, Dr. Anny Katan, Prof. Hans Kelsen, Mr. M. Masud Khan, Dr. Marianne Kris, Dr. Edward Kronold, Dr. Jeanne Lampl-de Groot, Prof. Harold Lasswell, Mrs. Elma Laurvik, Mrs. Kata Levy, Prof. Heinrich Meng, Dr. Emanuel Miller, Dr. Fritz Moellenhoff, Dr. Roger Money-Kyrle, Prof. Henry Murray, Dr. Herman Nunberg, Mrs. Ochsner, Dr. Sylvia Payne, Prof. Lionel Penrose, Dr. Irmarita Putnam, Dr. Marian C. Putnam, Dr. Sandor Rado, Mrs. Beata Rank, Dr. Annie Reich, Dr. Theodor Reik, Mrs. Eva Rosenfeld, Dr. Charles Rycroft, Mrs. Hanns Sachs, Dr. Philip Sarasin, Dr. Raymond Saussure, Dr. Melitta Schmideberg, Dr. Max Schur, Dr. Hannah Segal, Dr. Rene Spitz, Dr. Richard Sterba, Mr. & Mrs. James Strachey, Dr. John Sutherland, Dr. Marius Tausk, Dr. Victor Hugo Tausk, Mrs.

Nada Mascherano-Tausk, Dr. Alan Tyson, Mrs. Helene Velt-fort, Dr. Robert Waelder, Dr. Richard Wagner, Dr. Edoardo Weiss, Dr. & Mrs. George Wilbur, Dr. Donald Winnicott, Dr. Martha Wolfenstein, Mr. Leonard Woolf.

While many of these people were in one way or another intimately bound up with Freud, a few of them had met him only once, and some simply shared my interest in the beginnings of modern psychology. To all of them I am indebted for their cooperation.

As a coherent group they possessed common memories of a revolutionary past; they had once formed an underground movement at odds with the conventional wisdom of psychiatry, academic life, and, indeed, the more general beliefs of their time. It was no easy task to overcome their suspicions of a young outsider coming to study them. My own earlier manuscript on Freud was no doubt some help, as was my obvious respect for them: as disciples of Freud they had been a truly creative group. Their experiences also led me to reflect about the general relation of pupils to teachers, the ways in which one learns and grows, as well as the sources of the frustration and stifling of talent.

Some were so identified with the master that speaking with them gave the spooky impression of communing with Freud himself; they echoed his convictions, and even his phrasing of opinions. The exceptionally gentle and kindly souls were determined to put the best face on everything, as were the more politic among them. But at the other extreme the nastier types and the malcontents did not have a good word to say about anyone. A psychiatrist who will talk on about Freud's spittoon, for example, is likely to be sharp-tongued about everything. But each informant had something to teach.

I had to be on guard against being misled by the vagaries of human memory concerning the distant past. However, the old proverbially have more trouble remembering events a week ago than of fifty years ago. Memories of earlier and better days crowd an aging mind. Most of these people had already partially retired. The old need to review their lives. Aging, one weighs events to set things straight and even to atone for past mistakes. The old and the young have this one crucial tie in common—they each have nothing to lose.

In the middle of my interviewing I stumbled upon a treasure house of documents. Freud's daughter Anna, with her family's support, had commissioned Ernest Jones to write an authorized biography of her father. She has always maintained a tight, secretive hold on everything connected with Freud's life, even censoring his letters for publication. She scrutinized Jones's work line by line, while helping him in every way she could. Shortly after Jones completed his massive three-volumed biography, he died, and eventually his papers were shipped to a large cabinet in the basement of the London Institute of Psychoanalysis.

There they lay until I came upon them in the summer of 1965. Others had casually glanced through them, and some attempt had been made to sort them out. But no one had ever gone through them, scrap by scrap. These archives contained every piece that had gone into making up Freud's official biography. One could discover who had told Jones which bit of information and who had refused to help. Jones's private opinions and the exchanges with those who corresponded with him could be very lively, much more interesting than the solemn account which made its way into the biography itself.

When I set out in my research, nothing could have been further from my mind than uncovering the suppressed account of Victor Tausk's life and death. His story remains the most exciting I came across, and while I intend before long to publish a broader account of Freud, his patients, and his pupils, I have chosen to break off this tale about Freud and Tausk in order to ensure its being remembered.

"No one will tell you about Tausk!"—so I was told very early in my interviewing. That was all the tip-off I needed, and from then on I regularly asked people if or what they knew of Tausk, a figure previously unknown to me. The oldest analysts were incredulous that so little was known about Tausk's significance, and some younger ones were convinced that a secret surrounded him that more senior members of Freud's inner circle might be able to shed light on. From many I sensed an air of mystery about Tausk, and everyone familiar with his work testified to its importance. Finally Alfred Adler's daughter casually answered that she knew Tausk's son. After I contacted him, he sent me a copy of the suicide note his father had written to Freud the morning Tausk killed himself in 1919.

It would have been impossible for me to unravel this story, and succeed in my detective work, without the full cooperation of Tausk's family, his two sons and the surviving sister who was closest to him. Whatever his own troubles, he succeeded in arousing their lasting love and devotion. Tausk's own psychoanalyst also assisted my project, although her view of Tausk was necessarily a partial one.

No one could have known beforehand that it would ever be possible to reconstruct this tale, since no one had ever tried to fit all the pieces together. Jones himself, far from the Vienna scene, would have personally known little of the story, and if he had guessed the import of it would never have pursued the unsettling details. But the further I proceeded in my interviewing on the history of psychoanalysis, the more Tausk's life took hold of me. He was the first member of the Vienna Psychoanalytic Society to study the psychoses clinically, at a time when Freud himself was only interested in treating far less disturbed people. Tausk made some lasting contributions to modern psychoanalytic theory and psychotherapy which have been incorporated in the works of such contemporary thinkers as Bruno Bettelheim and Erik Erikson; but he could not survive in Freud's circle. He was a dashing Slav, whose dynamism and good looks won the hearts of a whole series of women, yet his marriage ended in failure and successive love affairs came to grief. A man of great versatility, a poet and a writer, a lawyer as well as a physician and psychoanalyst, Tausk was finally overwhelmed by his contact with Freud.

Tausk's struggle with Freud was misunderstood at the time and has since been repressed out of loyalty to the master. Understanding this conflict and why it has taken so long to become public should alter the standard picture of Freud. The two men formed an uncanny pair of opposites, as their strengths and frailties played into each other's hands. The story of their controversy, and Tausk's destruction, can serve as a vehicle for reinterpreting Freud's stature.

Henry Ford thought history was bunk, and the more one ponders how Tausk has been forgotten, the more one acquires a healthy skepticism about all written accounts of the past. When Tausk killed himself, he left instructions that all his papers be destroyed; it took a full day to burn them. Tausk wanted to be extinguished, and history has complied. Now, fifty years after his suicide, this account may help bring him back to life.

Brother Animal

psychological contributions can be made known. Fascinating as he was to contemporaries, Tausk's name is known today only among psychiatrists interested in early psychoanalytic papers. His rightful historical place, though, and the way in which he was finally crushed powerfully illustrate the timeless theme of how a man's struggle to liberate himself can end in his own undoing.

Any suicide may evoke horror and awe, as well as guilt in those who might have helped. In Tausk's instance all the normal reactions are intensified by his having been so well-trained a psychiatrist, one of Freud's most brilliant pupils. Tausk died at forty, in the midst of his most productive period. He had such immense capacities and was still so promising—concern with his story grows because of the incompleteness of his life. We can never know what he would have made of the rest of it. In the course of growing older each of us closes out many options and lives one life at the expense of others which are inconsistent with it. Contemplating another cut off in midstream, as we speculate on the alternative courses his life might have taken, we are tempted to imagine the variety of destinies that might once have been possible for ourselves as well.

This tale gives a fresh dimension to the past conflicts in psychoanalysis, for it helps us to understand what those dissensions meant from the point of view of Freud's pupils. The development of psychoanalysis cannot be told only from the perspective of Freud's own reactions to "defectors." Too often these struggles have been oversimplified and blamed solely on the difficulties of Freud's students.

To the extent that Tausk's place in history now exists, it

is mainly as one of Lou Andreas-Salomé's lovers. They had a short affair in Vienna, during her stay there in 1912–13. Years earlier in Lou's life the philosopher Nietzsche had reputedly proposed to her, and she had subsequently been intimate with the poet Rilke. When she came into Freud's circle to learn psychoanalysis, a woman like Lou would hardly waste herself on a nobody. Since she could not have Freud himself, Tausk, who had considerable talent and standing in Freud's eyes, represented second best. And in her *Journal* on Freud Tausk plays a key role. She in fact wrote the most penetrating comments on Tausk's character. Yet only if one knows the whole story are her observations on him comprehensible. Without all the background material, her dark and misty prose remains impenetrable.

The oral tradition on Tausk is fragmentary. To the generation of psychoanalysts who came after the First World War, Tausk is known as a genius who failed.[1] Of course any ingroup does tend to overestimate its own members, though some were more confident than others in their extremely high estimation of Tausk's abilities. Still, for those who became analysts in the 1920's and 1930's, while Freud was still alive, Tausk looms as a mythical figure from the past who died at the height of his powers. More rumors exist about how Tausk died than about why. Many know virtually nothing else about him except that he is supposed to have castrated himself.[2]

Among the older psychoanalysts who were already intimate with Freud at the time of Tausk's suicide, none can understand at all how he has been forgotten today. He figured so much in their own experience that they can scarcely believe his name may now mean absolutely nothing, even to someone relatively well-versed in psychoanalysis. One elderly analyst bragged about knowing Tausk. He stressed his acquaintance with Tausk and his knowledge of Tausk's career as a way of making himself more important to me as a source of information about the whole history of the movement.

Those who knew Tausk personally are still shocked at his suicide. Tausk was such an alive man, with so much imagination, and he had so many interests—*there* was a human life. To those who knew Tausk professionally, his suicide was very sudden and surprising. Freud himself composed the official obituary of Tausk.* "No one," he wrote, "could escape the impression that here was a man of importance." Freud's final judgment has become ironic: "He is sure of an honorable memory," Freud proclaimed, "in the history of psychoanalysis and its earliest struggles."[3] This three-page obituary is the lengthiest Freud ever penned. Although sheer quantity of words is no sure sign of someone's importance in Freud's eyes, he did write shorter obituaries about Karl Abraham, Lou Andreas-Salomé, Josef Breuer, and Sandor Ferenczi—each assuredly known to history books. It seems all the more remarkable that a figure like Tausk could have disappeared so completely.[4]

* Freud's obituary appears in full here in Chap. v, pp. 135–8.

No one in particular has been actively responsible for suppressing a full account of the difficulties between Freud and Tausk. But, as we shall later see, the letter from Freud to Lou Andreas-Salomé after Tausk's death has been tendentiously edited. It is not surprising if Freud's disciples in Vienna kept this story to themselves. We should remember their reverence for Freud, as well as their guilt over a fallen rival. A suicide under any circumstances is a fearful act. But coming after his fight with Freud, Tausk's suicide helped give a sense of reality to the powers that Freud's pupils magically attributed to their leader.

Quarreling with Freud was the most dreadful possibility imaginable. To be cast out by him meant expulsion from the chosen few, psychic death. The book would be closed, the candle snuffed out. Tausk's death substantiated all the fantasied consequences of struggling with Freud. It is easy to understand why events worked to keep this episode obscure.

Tausk's family had no inkling of his fight with Freud. It must have been a frightful business for Tausk, and he was apparently discreet about so important a matter in his life. Half a century later it proved news to his family to hear the first outlines of the controversy. They had, however, letters at their disposal. With the help of these documents, added to what could be learned from interviewing Tausk's family and colleagues, it has now become possible to reconstruct a reliable sequence of events.

Unearthing Tausk's story has had the fascination of a clinical riddle. The material unfolded as gradually as it might about a patient, and presenting it for readers poses essentially the problem of writing a case history. If only this detective work were not about Freud, he would have sympathized with it; the revolutionary in him always sought fresh interpretations of accepted knowledge. Moreover, besides upsetting conventional wisdom and solving a puzzle, the Tausk story also clarifies in a humanly satisfying way Freud's whole career.

2   *T*his is not a full-scale biography of Victor Tausk, but rather an examination of his life in relation to psychoanalysis. What aspects of Tausk's early life would be relevant to his involvement with Freud? He was born in Slovakia on March 12, 1879, in a town then called Zsilina. Shortly after birth he was taken to Croatia, now a part of Yugoslavia but in those days an outlying province of the Austro-Hungarian Empire, of which Vienna was the cultural center.

Victor was the eldest of nine children, with six sisters and two brothers. His German-speaking family was technically Jewish, but completely nonpracticing.[5] His father, Hermann Tausk, had worked first as a schoolteacher and then as an editor of a weekly newspaper in Zagreb. Hermann seems to have been highly intelligent and gifted, and soon became an internationally known journalist. He wrote in favor of the monarchy, attempting to explain the problems of Vienna to the Croatians and those of Croatia to the Viennese. Hermann delighted in adventure and could not live for a long time in the same way; so around 1892 he moved his family to Sarajevo, becoming chief of the press office of the Government of Bosnia and Herzegovina. (Bosnia, today a part of Yugoslavia, then had only recently been taken from the Turks.) A full-time journalist in addition to his official duties, Hermann Tausk was editor of his own journal and a correspondent for several foreign newspapers and periodicals.

Victor's mother, Emilie Roth Tausk, seems to fit the archetypal pattern of the masochistic Jewish mother who gives everything for others. To her aggressive and even tyrannical husband she responded with self-sacrifice and family devotion. Hermann was not a good provider, so she always had to accept money from her own mother. Although Emilie is reported to have been beautiful, her constant anxieties and demands for her children left her tired and cheerless, and her husband was unfaithful. Hermann was a restless man, sometimes in need of a journey to quiet his spirits. Yet he could be quite charming and women found him fascinating.

Victor was on the whole a tender and thoughtful son to his mother, and in later years she followed his psychoanalytic writings. Emilie appears to have been as large-hearted as Hermann was authoritarian—and Victor took something from both into his personality. His relationship to his father was strained and antagonistic. Victor later wrote that he was forever embarrassed to be called by his father's name. Hermann, a hard-working and popular man, found he always had opposition at home, and it was led by his eldest son.

Whatever Hermann's own sexual behavior, he expected his children to be hypermoral. On moralistic grounds, for example, he broke up his eldest daughter's engagement to a fine young man, with whom she was very much in love. (The suitor—out of generosity and correctness—was paying support for an illegitimate child whose true father was indeterminate.) Hermann loved scenes and sentiment, using his theatricality to support his own need for authority at home. He would dramatize self-pityingly his family's impertinent treatment of him as an outsider. Victor grew up, then, with the model of a father who misbehaved toward his own wife, and who as a Bosnian official opposed the growing national feeling for Yugoslavia among the young.

In school Victor learned to speak perfect Croatian, although his mother had never deigned to learn it at all. He studied Latin, Greek, became a talented linguist, and later displayed a good command of French and Italian. Admired by his fellow students, he was a leader among them in behalf of justice and intelligence. He had a row with a teacher of religion whose principles conflicted with his own atheism; just before graduating he led a strike over religion at school, and so finished getting his matura at Varaždin. A period of ill health—lung trouble—did not interfere with his plans to attend the University of Vienna.

At first he had wanted to study medicine, but since his family could not afford it, he settled on the less expensive prospect of becoming a lawyer.

In 1897 Tausk went to Vienna, where the next year he met his future wife, Martha Frisch, a distant relative of Martin Buber, the theologian and philosopher. Although Victor's family was cultured, by Viennese standards he was still a raw provincial. His hostile relationship to his father apparently extended to his future father-in-law, a printer in Vienna; they passionately hated each other.

Martha fell in love with Victor over her family's objections. Like Victor she was ambitious. Intellectual women were rare in those days, and Martha seems to have felt that as an intellectual and convinced Marxist she had to despise her femininity, not dress well, and in general she downgraded the importance of sexuality. She was very intelligent, though rather theatrical, and later on became an active socialist, speaking, debating, writing articles, and attending conferences. But she was a more rigid person than her future husband, with fewer capacities. At any rate she loved Victor deeply, became pregnant, and they were married in 1900.* Victor was twenty-one, and Martha almost two years younger. Together they went back to Yugoslavia, where the baby died at birth.

---

* As Martha was a Christian, though her father a Jew, Tausk was baptized before his marriage. He always continued later on, however, to acknowledge his Jewishness; and few people knew of his formal conversion.[6]

In Sarajevo Victor continued his training as a lawyer. When Martha gave birth to a son (Marius) in 1902, Victor already had his doctorate in jurisprudence. A little less than two years later they had another son, Victor Hugo. The names of the two children represent the way Martha, and to some extent Victor, felt about being in Sarajevo. She did not want to give her sons German names, lest they suffer while in Croatia; nor did she want to give them Croatian names, since she hoped someday to return to what she considered a civilized country. Meanwhile, as part of his training, Victor had begun to act as a judge.

In 1904 Tausk took his family to Mostar, where he practiced as a lawyer's assistant. Tausk enjoyed defending the penniless, especially murderers. In one case, a Moslem girl had been arrested for killing her illegitimate child. Although the prosecutor asked for the death penalty, Victor was so eloquent in defending her that she was acquitted. Reactionary ideas, he argued, had been at fault, and these false notions had forced her to kill her child. In the spring of 1905 he attained a "stalum agendi," which meant that he could serve as one of the limited number of full-fledged lawyers. Had Tausk gone on in the law, he would have been sent to Derventa, where he was assured of a lucrative practice.

But instead, late in the spring of 1905, Martha and Victor decided to separate. With the two children they went to Vienna, where Martha eventually got a job as a bookkeeper in her father's firm. By early 1906 Victor had settled in Berlin. From that time on numerous letters exist from Victor to Martha, which she faithfully preserved until her death in 1957. He sent her money whenever possible, always inquired about their boys, and sometimes bitterly reproached her for the failure of their marriage.

One letter in particular strikingly communicates Tausk's feelings at this stage of his life. It sounds almost like an entry meant for a diary. Tausk was then twenty-six, married and the father of two children, and he had been stuck away in the provinces for several years. In this letter of August 11, 1905, he relates how a friend had criticized his restlessness and ambition, charging that

I have no right to act the way I do. It isn't my business to look for new paths but to provide for my children. Formerly he thought there was an exceptional law for me. Now he says that Victor Tausk is just a man like any other and he has to do his duty. How deeply his words have touched me. If he were right that would be terrible. Why shouldn't I be able to try? I have not really tried anything in my life. I have immediately been pressed into a mold. I am vacillating between desire and duty. I can't give up the hope that what I desire together with my good abilities will ultimately set sail from the harbor. I know all the objections but I shall try.

As his marriage began to break up, Tausk had turned to writing. He published some Serbian ballads which he had translated into German. His talents were partly directed to working over his own dilemmas. For example, he wrote a Bosnian gypsy tale, "Husein Brko," which was published in his father's journal. This beautiful, well-controlled story tells of a man without attachments who becomes a thief and a murderer. The theme of the homelessness of the gypsies and the primitive impulses released by the absence of a structured life reflects Tausk's anxiety and distress at the collapse of his marriage and the abandonment of his profession. Ultimately, Husein is slain by his own father. The tale was based on an actual court case, yet it foreshadows Tausk's fate with Freud as well.

Tausk also tried his hand as a playwright, though his work was never performed. His play was obviously autobiographical, but he was simultaneously testing his talent as a writer. By July 1905 in Vienna he completed "Twilight"; its protagonist gives up his "position" and goes into "uncertainty" for the sake of his own better self, and for art. It is all written with the self-seriousness characteristic of a major German tradition. The hero, Wolfgang, is exactly Tausk's age, and has two sons. In the play, and perhaps in life, his wife encourages him to believe he is no ordinary man, and that he must get out of the "colony" for the sake of his talent.

"I must dig out my better self," Wolfgang exclaims, "before it is too late." He has "never really dared anything. Everything has moved by its own momentum." Wolfgang blames his father for considering his artistic side only a diversion. On the one hand, Wolfgang has not been given enough guidance, on the other, he has been misled. "They drove me into this profession which I have never liked because you can make a living in it earlier." Wolfgang's strivings to find himself conflict with his overwhelming sense of duty. Wringing his hands, he despairingly abandons his family.

In his new *vie bohème* he is surrounded by an array of admiring men and women whose belief in his multifold talents does not help alleviate his guilt. For this breath of freedom he is severely punished, and significantly at first by the disaster that he somehow brings upon others. His wife's young brother commits suicide under the influence of Wolfgang's nihilistic belief in the meaninglessness of life, and his two sons die of consumption. Ultimately, however, he is able to build triumph from despair and writes a play recounting the tragedy of his marriage which brings him some sense of fulfillment and justification even at the moment of his death, also from consumption.

These themes reflect Tausk's most immediate preoccupations, especially his guilt, one reason why the play is terribly tedious. Wolfgang is so self-absorbed in his own troubles that it is hard to believe the other characters in the play could have cared to listen to him.

In Berlin Tausk was able to embark on the new career he longed for. Employing his multiple gifts, he wrote poetry, practiced his violin, drew charcoal sketches, and directed plays. There was some basis for his aspiration to be a universal genius. The necessity of earning a living, however, forced him to struggle at journalism, which for him was degrading. In all his letters to Martha in Vienna we find his efforts to earn money, his yearning for creative work, as well as his concern for his boys. Although she had been deeply hurt by him, Martha never turned her sons against their father. Whatever her complaints or her own sense of failure as a woman, at the bottom of her heart she loved him to the end of her life.

3 *R*eflecting on Tausk's career change just before fully qualifying as a lawyer, it seems doubtful that he needed to make such a radical break with his past. He certainly had not exhausted the possibilities for fulfilling work in the profession he had already prepared for. But for Tausk law had been merely the shortest and cheapest academic study leading to a professional title. Apparently he complained about not wanting to defend scoundrels; certainly money-making was not enough for him. Tausk later wrote that he was unwilling to be an officer of a court. Young and talented, his aspirations left him disappointed with the life of a lawyer. In Berlin, though, having started a new life, he found himself in a struggle for survival. He wrote reviews, and even whistled in cafés. But he always had financial difficulties.

Reading other people's mail can be a pleasurable form of snooping, but the letters to Martha in Vienna are painful even after so many years. One letter in particular, however, illuminates the failure of his marriage, as well as his future tie to Freud. In "Twilight" Wolfgang had complained that his wife's love had been a burden. The problem with Tausk's marriage was not just that he had deceived his true self by becoming a lawyer, and consequently had behaved badly out of self-hatred. In addition Tausk seems to have been unable to tolerate his wife's dependent love; for Victor, Martha had not been self-sufficient enough to make him comfortable with her.

I love only free people, those that are independent of me. For those who depend upon me make me dependent—for this I revenge myself, and then become guilty towards those who did me good. The guilt however eats up the capital, because it bears negative interest of immeasurable dimensions if one wants to pay one's debts. One cannot be bankrupt too often—I have at any rate already lost much of my credit. I want to work my way up in such a way as my nature requires, without fostering false ambitions and ambiguous feelings. Only in this way shall I be able to gain moral capital. The way I am living now is truly the best one for this intention: independent because nobody depends on me, not a slave because not a master.*

Tausk understood the destructive element in his great capacity to love. The more he loved, the more dependent he became, and hence by the curious logic of his emotions, also the more cruel. Perhaps as a reaction to this aggressive part of him, throughout his life he gave to others, was good-hearted, devoted, and loyal. But when he suddenly realized how enslaved he had become, he would

* March 1, 1906.

break the relationship, and the whole cycle would begin again with someone else.

Most of his letters from Berlin are less revealing of his character, except for the self-pity. But as with Wolfgang in "Twilight," had this been all there was to Tausk he would never have won Martha in the first place, nor could he have gone on as he did to arouse the deep love and devotion of so many beautiful and talented women throughout his life. Complaining to Martha about all his troubles, telling her his worst torments, he was perhaps unconsciously blaming her. But doubtless another factor was at work as well. Later we shall see that during this stay in Berlin he had a very happy love affair; since Tausk had abandoned Martha, he could scarcely write of the happiest parts of his new life. By not appearing to be enjoying himself at Martha's expense, he could ease his guilt toward her. If he appeared to his wife as a miserable wretch, then he had never denied her anything he was capable of giving.

The day after his twenty-seventh birthday he wrote that "my heart is so tired, that I would rather not be in this world."[*] He could appeal for her love through a display of his suffering, and thereby also expiate guilt. Of course it is always hard to distinguish the genuine depressive feelings from the general air of romanticism. Occasionally he wrote about happy events, his music or his sketching. But mainly he wrote about his feelings of loneliness and depression. "I am quite lonely and can not communicate with anybody—being a communicative person par excellence

[*] March 13, 1906.

—and therefore I miss an elevation of my feeling of my personality."*

In Berlin Tausk's health was gradually undermined. He longed for the sunny Dalmatian coast, where he had gone once before to cure his lungs. He secured a free place at a German sanatorium, Ahrweiler on the Rhine, in exchange for a promise to write a few promotional articles about it. On September 19, 1907, he announced to Martha his intention of getting a "physical and mental cleaning and strengthening." (A sanatorium was a private clinic for treating physical and nervous illnesses—not, as an American today might guess, a lunatic asylum.) In addition to his relapse of lung trouble, he complained to his wife of fatigue and lack of concentration. But he hoped to be able to write something beautiful while recuperating.

On September 27 he had his initial medical examination. The diagnosis was mental and physical exhaustion. He was told that he had a "hereditary inclination towards the psychopathological side," whatever that might mean. He hastened to assure his wife that his life was not in danger. "What would help me is money, pleasure, and success. The heart is nervous, the lung has a catarrh . . . I must get a clear head and control of my nerves. Then I can give shape to my life."†

His mind was troubled, but he felt sure his sense of

* March 20, 1906.
† September 27, 1907.

mastery would return. Unexpectedly, his condition deteriorated rapidly. As in Thomas Mann's novel, only upon seeking to improve his health on a "magic mountain" did he find himself truly ill. Tausk's guilt feelings were mobilized; his sadism was converted into masochism, and he slid into a depression. Two days after his medical examination he wrote Martha that "one can be more alone than alone." He began to sound desperate in searching for a way out of his dilemmas. He feared he would get worse without the help of some "mentally normal . . . wise and good human being." He was searching for "salvation," a way of life in which "your heart gets richer because you can daily practice the duties of love towards genuine and kind human beings."* He yearned for a profession and a home, but had neither.

The next day he felt even worse. Psychiatrically he was not so badly off that he could not still pour out his troubles to his wife. He functioned admirably as a writer describing what it means not to function. A depression characteristically sharpens self-awareness, which is precisely why this affliction can be so painful to watch. It is a far cry from the self-congratulation of a man fancying he is Napoleon. Tausk's inner world was troubled, and he teetered on the edge of an abyss.

I go for walks, and I am trying again to feel nature. In those last twenty months in Berlin, there have been strange changes in me; I have lost the feeling for nature. I am incurably ill in

* September 29, 1907.

my soul. My whole past appears to me to be nothing but a preparation for this terrible collapse of my personality. If I have never believed in the power of the blood, now I believe that a human being gets his fate from his parents. Nevertheless, I'm still struggling, and trying again to become strong and independent. But I'm groping around in the dark . . . One needs a guide. The doctor tells me, "people like you thrive and live brilliantly in a normal and secure situation. Then they are useful and a joy to themselves and to others. If one takes away the base they are used to, they simply collapse." Hereditary unfitness for life. . . . Last night my head was working clearly and productively. I wrote fifteen pages on the metaphysics of the art of acting. But I cannot work continuously. The nerves are playing, the head gets tired. However, all gets healthier. My color is good. My weight is increasing. What will become of the boys? I am desolate. Everything depends on money—happiness and life.

Later that day his spirits improved, and he added to the letter he had already written:

A true neurasthenic becomes clear-headed in the evening. I took a wonderful walk through the night landscape. The country is indescribably beautiful. Only the doctors have intelligent faces. The patients all look like poisoned rats and mules. All destroyed faces—such destroyed faces. I don't get any treatment. I take a bath at 10 in the evening for my insomnia. Not much success so far. Chiefly I go for walks and I'm drinking milk. Apart from the prescribed ration of a liter and a half per day, on my walks I drink another liter in various restaurants out of private diligence. I'm scared of writing articles. . . . My lung is improving. For the last six weeks I've been coughing in competition with my sons. I shouldn't write such long letters—the doctor told me not to—he told me to be lazy.*

The next few days must have been harrowing. Tausk's symptoms appeared to be those of a classic depression— self-reproaches, sleep disturbances, along with anxieties of impoverishment. He was eating himself up with grief. For a few days he could not write to Martha, and then on October 4 he told her how he had been in bed for two days,

with a completely troubled brain, physically and mentally so tired that I could not do the simplest work. For months I haven't known what it is to get enough sleep. And since I've been here I don't even know what sleep means. As of today I have to take a sleeping drug, since the hydrotherapy fails. Surely I will do what I can. I'm quite helpless and alone. And I don't even know what I shall eat when I get back to Berlin.

He mentioned the chance of getting a well-paying newspaper job in Hanover. But he felt he could not work, and that was "the terrible thing. I'm completely ruined." By October 9 he was still deeply disturbed, yet wonderfully affectionate about his little boys.

Gradually the whole illness comes out. Obsessional ideas, heavy depressions, pressure in my head, and tired, tired. Six months of treatment is a minimum to get on my legs again. What a year this has been. Desperate plans [for a trip to Yugoslavia]. Everything is ill and without guidance.

---

* September 30, 1907.

Tausk's collapse had come on sudden and unexpectedly, and his recovery was equally rapid and spontaneous. The worst period had lasted about two weeks. He stayed in the sanatorium just a little over three weeks. On October 11 he wrote about leaving bed: "I'm getting better. Now it remains to be seen whether my depressions will be lasting and periodic. The doctor thinks they will recur several times. In the meantime I have stopped taking sleeping drugs." Although he still felt exhausted and disturbed, his letters describe a steady recuperation, and he left the sanatorium on October 22, 1907.

These letters establish the nature of Tausk's difficulties. His collapse evolved from his physical illness as well as the inner turmoil of preceding years. The letters document his sense of failure and helplessness, his shame at being unable to take care of his children. The depressive emotions, though never again that debilitating, recurred to plague him. He felt he would "go to pieces" unless he got a job soon, even if it had to be in Vienna. During the next month he wrote Martha from Berlin that he did not have the "courage to think truly of the future. It will be better to live the future down, as I have been living down through all my crazy futures."* He felt like a "sunk human being . . . physically, mentally and financially put out of action. . . . Life has not shaped me, it has crushed me. I'm an ugly powerless mass, deadly tired, and I have had enough of this life."†

* November 10, 1907.
† November 29, 1907.

But Tausk was still only twenty-eight years old. Any original person is likely to have conflicts and anxieties which exceed the range of the statistically normal, and for a sensitive and talented young man who, though already a lawyer and an accomplished journalist, has not yet found fulfilling work, the situation was bound to be particularly frustrating. Passions and great suffering are frequently accepted as the cost of creativity. Tausk's life in Berlin had left him run-down and exhausted; no matter how hard he struggled, he could not rise above the most insecure existence. But despite this interlude of intense self-deprecation, his self-confidence was not so deeply shaken that his ambitions would let him compromise yet.

For Tausk had courage; even after such a terrible collapse, he could pick himself up and decide to try something new. Out of this misery he turned to Freud and psychoanalysis. Before going to Vienna, however, Tausk made a trip to Italy; a glowing letter to Martha records his full recovery.* In Freud he sought to find all the guidance he had so sorely lacked. According to Tausk's youngest sister, he responded to an article of Freud's with a letter. Freud, thinking Tausk was a medical doctor, encouraged him to come to Vienna to study psychoanalysis. While Tausk's life improved vastly over the next few years, his past deep unhappiness explains how he could fear the collapse of the new existence he proceeded to build up.

Martha was having a difficult time in Vienna, but at least she had a secure, if small, income from the position

* September 19, 1908.

in her father's firm. The two children continued to thrive. In the fall of 1908 Tausk came to Vienna to study medicine; he already planned to become a psychoanalyst. While studying he would hold a job on a Viennese newspaper. Before beginning anew once again, he determined to put an end to a part of his former life: although he and Martha had been separated ever since October 1905, only on his return to Vienna in October 1908 did they go through with a divorce.

4 *H*istorical perspective is necessary to understand what it meant to become a psychoanalyst in 1909. Unlike nowadays in the United States, where psychoanalysis has become so widely accepted, the field was not then a recognized profession, and people had to come to it via their own introspection and dedication. Freud's career was at a phase when his extreme isolation was over, and pupils had begun to gather about him. The turning point, Freud later thought, had come in 1906 or 1907.[7] Even so, by the beginning of 1909 the Vienna Psychoanalytic Society had only twenty-eight members, and it was unusual for more than eight or ten to come to meetings.

The impersonal-sounding word "psychoanalysis" in fact then meant Freud personally. It would have been inconceivable to embark on its study, especially in Vienna, without some personal encouragement from Freud himself. Actually, Freud never had a very high opinion of his early group in Vienna. He complained of having a "heavy cross to bear with the older generation" of Viennese analysts.[8] But, as Freud explained it in 1914, "in view of the courage displayed by their devotion to a subject so much frowned upon and so poor in prospects, I was disposed to tolerate much among the members to which I should otherwise have made objection."[9]

Tausk had Freud's personal support, and the rest of the Viennese psychoanalytic group did what they could to smooth his way. It was immediately obvious to all of them that he had very superior abilities. With the advantages of hindsight, his choosing to become a psychoanalyst may seem a temporary life-saving operation. But it was also a natural outgrowth of his talents and interests. Tausk had always possessed the psychological gifts of a born understander. And people with manic-depressive tendencies are capable of being in excellent contact with other human beings.

Freud's encouragement meant everything to Tausk at the time. Besides sending him patients, Freud helped Tausk directly with loans of money. Freud was characteristically very generous this way, always living quite modestly himself. He gave money at various times to Lou Andreas-Salomé, Theodor Reik, Otto Rank, Hanns Sachs, as well as to a favorite patient, the "Wolfman." There were no doubt other instances. Freud used money impersonally, for the sake of the cause. It is not clear how much Freud advanced Tausk, but we do know that four of Freud's pupils in Vienna (Hitschmann, Federn, Jekels, and Steiner) gave Tausk four thousand kronen, worth about eight hundred dollars at that time. At the end of the summer of 1909 Tausk wrote to his former wife that Freud had just sent him 150 kronen, but that it was not enough to finance his planned vacation. "What is going to come now only Freud and God know."*

Tausk was not the only pupil of Freud's to abandon his previous profession to become a psychoanalyst. That whole early generation of psychoanalysts typically came to Freud with the bravado of a frustrated or failed career. Freud encouraged both Sachs (a lawyer) and Reik (a scholar), for example, to give up their previous fields, and to practice psychoanalysis for the sake of understanding its theory. As a profession psychoanalysis was hazardous. But with the support of Freud and his circle an analyst could rely on at least a few patients being sent regularly. Paradoxically, even today, if there are fifty colleagues in one city a psychoanalyst's income is more secure than if there are only two or three. So as psychoanalysis began to take hold, its prospects as a career brightened, and unlike many professions, it could be practiced anywhere.

Tausk was exceptional in moving so quickly from being a patient with emotional difficulties of his own, no matter how transitory, to being a therapist himself. But the fantasy of becoming an analyst must have at least entered the head of every psychological patient with a minimum de-

*August 31, 1909.

gree of intelligence. Even today psychiatry as a field tends to attract people who are busy with themselves. In those early days of psychoanalysis, however, it took someone at odds with himself to be able to see the relevance of Freud, despite the barriers of convention.

The personal circumstances under which Tausk made this new career change were especially difficult, for he always felt obliged to help Martha and the boys in every way he could. Tausk might seem to have made his life unnecessarily difficult by studying medicine: assuming it made sense to become a psychoanalyst, was it not a surplus burden also to become a physician? Probably not, for though Freud later wrote a pamphlet maintaining the feasibility of laymen's practicing psychoanalysis, in the years before World War I his writings take for granted that the psychoanalyst will also be a doctor.[10] Freud certainly harbored a strong wish to triumph in the medical world. If a follower could bring with him the respect of the medical profession, and of hospital psychiatry in particular, then he would be all the more useful to the advancement of psychoanalysis. Certainly other disciples of Freud's before World War I became doctors in order to practice psychoanalysis.[11]

The circle around Freud included almost as many literary and humanistic students as it did members of the medical fraternity; but though these laymen were people of very high standards, and Freud's teachings were a revelation for them, none of them were practicing psychoanalysis at that time. Those who were doctors tended to be general practitioners and internists rather than trained psychiatrists. Neurologists like Freud saw mainly ambulatory cases.

In Vienna of that era neurologists specialized in impairments of sensation and movement, due to infection, injury, or other damage to the brain, spinal cord, and nerve trunks. Freud's great discovery, and the central contribution of psychoanalysis, lay in the realm of psychogenic disorders—those syndromes of inappropriate behavior not referable to brain or spinal cord lesions. As a psychologist Freud set out to understand the most general laws of mental functioning.

When Tausk became a doctor, then, he may from the outset have envisioned a special role for himself, for unlike Freud and most of his medical following, Tausk chose to become a psychiatrist. It is important to realize that the psychoanalysts of those days, including Freud himself, had very little experience with hospitalized mental patients, who were seen only by psychiatrists. This point may be obscure from the contemporary American perspective, where psychoanalysts are—aside from a minority of lay analysts—psychiatrists first, with full medical credentials; but the early distinction between psychiatrists and psychoanalysts persists today throughout most of Europe. In England, for example, approximately a third of the analysts are nonmedical, and even doctors who are analysts as a rule have little status in psychiatry. The gulf between psychiatry, with its preoccupations with the psychotic, and psychoanalysis, which treats the less ill, needs to be under-lined if we are to appreciate the scope of Tausk's ambitions and accomplishments. For his most original achievements were to be his clinical studies of schizophrenia and manic-depressive insanity.

Psychoanalytic treatment was designed to cure neurotic patients. While neurosis in those days included a wider range of problems than it would now, even then it at-tempted to exclude the most seriously disturbed among the mentally ill. It was the Swiss, especially Jung and Bleuler, who came from within academic psychiatry to psycho-analysis. (Unlike the Viennese, the Swiss never made much of the distinction between neurology and psychi-atry.) Until Jung joined the movement just a couple of years before Tausk, Freud had no access to psychiatric material.[12]

When a Swiss psychiatrist came for a visit to the Vienna Psychoanalytic Society in 1910, for example, he found "about 30 persons . . . present. . . . [N]ot one of them was an academic psychiatrist. . . . I was struck by the lack of psychiatric training in the majority of the participants, even though there were very few beginners [in psycho-analysis] present; they had not even mastered the termi-nology [of psychiatry]."[13] The Swiss adherents mattered so much to Freud precisely because they promised new territory for his concepts to conquer in psychiatry. We shall return to the whole problem of the relation of early psychoanalytic thinking to the psychoses when evaluating the substance of Tausk's scientific work. But from the very outset of his involvement with Freud, Tausk was intimately associated with medical psychiatry.

Although the leaders in the Viennese academic world of psychiatry and neurology were by no means friendly to Freud's ideas, the younger people were often fascinated by them. So Tausk, with all his interest in psychoanalysis, also had a post at Frankl von Hochwart's neurological out-patient clinic. ("Clinic" was then the equivalent of our academic "department.") Throughout his years of studying medicine, Tausk remained part of Freud's inner circle.

Tausk also worked at the psychiatric clinic of the University of Vienna, headed by Professor Wagner von Jauregg. Wagner-Jauregg and Freud had a very complicated personal relationship. They were contemporaries, and had known each other since their school days. At the time Tausk was studying at this clinic, Wagner-Jauregg held the most prestigious psychiatric position in the Austro-Hungarian Empire. (He was Krafft-Ebing's successor.) Freud delivered his Saturday evening lectures, as a matter of fact, in Wagner-Jauregg's auditorium. (As long as Freud had an audience of three, he was entitled to lecture; but he always resented never being a regular faculty member.)

One of Wagner-Jauregg's later innovations was malarial treatment for general paresis, for which in 1927 he became the first and only psychiatrist ever to win a Nobel Prize.

But even before this a basis existed for rivalry between Wagner-Jauregg and Freud, as each of them had claim to fame. Wagner-Jauregg's assistants tended to be extremely antagonistic to Freud's work, and Freud grew very sensitive to any slights from Wagner-Jauregg's direction. For example, in the 1920's Freud was initially suspicious of Heinz Hartmann, now the dean of analysts in America, because he came from Wagner-Jauregg's clinic.

Although organically oriented, Wagner-Jauregg was a very sensitive psychiatrist. It was possible to be humane, though not a Freudian. On rounds he remembered which patient was suffering the most and went there first. He was as much a clinician as a scientist. Though humanly interested in patients, and respecting Freud personally, he considered psychoanalysis quite another matter. Wagner-Jauregg objected that Freud thought psychoanalysis could do everything.[14] In his stand as a psychiatrist against Freud, Wagner-Jauregg was perhaps more mocking than aggressively hostile; in other words, he maintained a tolerant but sarcastic attitude toward psychoanalysis. Although he could be biting, he was fair, and he certainly let his assistants do as they wanted about Freud. This psychiatric climate of opinion surrounding Freud is essential background for understanding Tausk's whole career.

The best source on Tausk's relationship to Freud's group before World War I remains Lou Andreas-Salomé's *Journal*.[15] Entirely aside from the "Tausk problem," Lou ranks as one of the subtlest interpreters of Freud's character and work. Indeed, the connection between Lou and Freud must interest anyone concerned with intellectual history. As Nietzsche's friend and expositor, she came to Freud with the aura of past European culture. Lou was still on close terms with Rilke, whose lover she had been and whose development as a poet she had assisted. Together they had taken a trip to Russia, where they made Tolstoy's acquaintance. (Lou introduced Rilke to Freud in 1913.)[16]

Lou was fifty-one when she came to Vienna in 1912; she regarded it as "the turning point" of her life.[17] Perhaps not entirely by chance, Freud also later wrote that 1912 had been "the very climax of my psychoanalytic work."[18] Before entering the Viennese psychoanalytic scene, she prepared herself by reading everything Freud had written. She came with the intention of eliciting Freud's interest in her, and succeeded completely in her aim.

Lou fits the genre of women who have a knack for collecting great men. Madame de Staël in the late eighteenth and early nineteenth centuries, and Alma Mahler in the twentieth illustrate the type. In Lou's case beauty was not her main attraction. Whatever her earlier good looks, she now had to rely on her psychological resources to arouse the attention of any potential conquests. Vibrantly responsive to ideas, Lou possessed an extraordinary flair for identifying with men, and especially with that creative part of them most subject to inner uncertainties. So of course she would read all of Freud before presenting herself to him.

Although Lou was useful to her line of great men precisely because she could identify with that most precious portion of themselves so in need of support, as men fell in love with her they eventually discovered that she had not truly given of herself. She had mirrored them, had helped their creative need, but at bottom Lou withheld herself as a person. Her great men all needed her, but each of her lovers ultimately realized how she had eluded him.

CHAPTER II

Zeus

1   In 1912, Freud at the age of fifty-six headed a family of six children. A physical relationship with Lou Salomé was out of the question, if only because Freud could never have tolerated the degree of disorder such an affair would entail. Freud was a nineteenth-century gentleman, in whom the eighteenth-century intellectual heritage prevailed. Just as his mind was systematic and meticulous, his manner was restrained, dignified, ceremonious, almost petit-bourgeois in its correctness. His enunciation was absolutely clear, and he spoke like a book. Always immaculately dressed, middle class though nonetheless striking in appearance, Freud was a man with his life well under control.

His daily routine proceeded with almost clocklike regularity. In bed at a routine hour and rising at an accustomed time, Freud had only to enter the suite of rooms adjacent to his apartment to receive his patients. They came and went for treatment and consultation, and they all knew he expected them to be punctual for their hour. Polite and well-controlled, Freud could be unassuming and quite natural in his office, which was strikingly cluttered with a collection of antique statuary. Between patients Freud usually went for a walk through the family apartment, before sitting down once more to listen to human troubles.

Though slender and medium-sized (five feet seven inches), Freud was a man of great presence. His eyes were almost melodramatic: deep-brown, even from photographs they seem to pierce through all sham and illusion. A portrait of Freud was once painted during a short period when he was clean-shaven; it looks nothing like the Freud history books have familiarized us with. But if one covers up the portion of that painting where his beard usually grew, then those burning, almost stinging eyes remind us immediately of the founder of psychoanalysis. Freud was an alive man, and his energy found expression not just in his work but in his walking, his impatience and restlessness, as well as in his almost continuous smoking. In the course of a single day he would consume about twenty cigars.

Although Freud was urbane and ironic, his eyes remind us how he could hate. The world's stupidity can be a terrible weight on anyone who sets out to think through everything anew. Freud saw it as his task to "disturb the peace of this world."[1] As he wrote to his fiancée long before he had made his mark, "I have often felt as though I had inherited all the defiance and all the passions with which our ancestors defended their Temple and could gladly sacrifice my life for one great moment in history."*[2] Freud's belligerence was an expression of his courage and independence. He was less persecuted for his ideas than his intransigence might suggest; rather he resented not yet having the world's recognition to which he felt entitled. Freud was a powerful man, no ordinary human being.

As early as Freud's adolescence one can find letters showing his inner awareness of his genius, as well as his determination to fulfill his immortality. Addressing the Vienna Psychoanalytic Society in his full maturity in the spring of 1912, just before Lou Andreas-Salomé came on the scene, Freud identifies himself as an agent of destiny:

If in the end I am convicted of being in error over the theoretical problems . . . I shall be able to console myself with the advance in our knowledge, which must disregard the opinions of an individual. You may then ask why, since I have such a laudable appreciation of the limitation of my own infallibility, I do not at once give in to these new suggestions but prefer to re-enact the familiar comedy of an old man obstinately clinging to his opinions. My reply is that I do not yet see any evidence to induce me to give in. In early days I made a number of alterations in my views and did not conceal them from the public. I was reproached on account of these changes, just as to-day I am reproached for my conservativeness. Not

* For Freud's relation to Judaism, cf. my *Freud: Political and Social Thought*, pp. 167–92.

that I should be intimidated by the one reproach or the other. But I know that I have a destiny to fulfill. I cannot escape it and I need not move towards it. I shall await it. . . .[3]

One might never guess from this how tiny a group Freud was addressing! It was also characteristic of Freud to begin so cautiously and then reveal that what lay behind such tact was nothing less than utter certainty. Freud was proud, but he had been able to transpose his vanity onto the movement he led. As early as 1903 he was writing about himself in the third person.

By the time of this speech, Freud's public life was well on the way to swallowing up his private life. At home the family revolved around him and his work. Although the Freuds might have guests, they never gave parties. Freud was not a mixer. The apartment was unusually quiet, especially considering the size of the family. As much as he peered into the depths of human motives in his office, at home he turned it all off completely. "In our house no one speaks of nerves," Freud's wife used to say.[4]

She was, like Tausk's wife, named Martha, but there the similarity ends. She and Freud had had a proper Victorian courtship, with a betrothal that lasted over a period of four years. From the letters between Freud and his future bride we know how demanding and possessive he could be. At one point he wanted her to break with members of her family, although at the time he himself was financially unprepared to assume responsibility for her. "I am afraid I do have a tendency towards tyranny," he admitted more than once.[5]

Frau Professor, as Freud's wife came to be called, was composed yet spirited, and put her husband on a pedestal. She enjoyed every bit of his becoming world famous. She had a wry sense of humor, and probably understood more of her husband's work than his pupils have cared to think.

Martha was certainly depreciated within the family, however, as the years went on and she grew old. Although she devoted herself to her husband, she was a fussy housewife, always cleaning up spots in the house, and preoccupied with where his cigar ashes might land. Much of Freud's own fastidiousness must have come from Martha's compulsive orderliness: she laid out his clothes, chose everything for him down to his handkerchiefs, and even put toothpaste on his toothbrush. Entertaining would have overwhelmed her with petty anxieties. Raising six children wore her out early, but before then her sister Minna had come to live with them. The two women fulfilled the household and child-raising tasks harmoniously. As large as Martha was delicate, and the more intellectual of the two, Minna became a much greater support to Freud in his work than her sister.

Evidently sexual relations between Freud and his wife came to an early end. By the age of forty-one he was writing to his most intimate friend that "sexual excitation is of no more use to a person like me."[6] In a bizarre attempt to overcome his cancer at the age of sixty-seven, Freud underwent a rejuvenatory operation on his testicles

(Steinach operation), but without benefit.* Freud's authorized biographer treated these matters with the utmost tact. The Steinach operation was camouflaged as the "ligature of the vas deferens on both sides."[7] And Jones mentioned in passing that "the more passionate side of married life subsided with him earlier than it does with many men. . . ."[8] In Freud's book on Leonardo, which contains many other autobiographical hints, Freud saw his hero as "a man whose sexual need and activity were exceptionally reduced, as if a higher aspiration had raised him above the common animal need of mankind."[9]

Freud's potency may have been influenced by his dislike of contraceptives. And since Martha was very easily impregnated, failing to withdraw was apt to mean children, which was bound to make the couple more anxious about intercourse. Just a year before Freud wrote that letter about sexuality being of no more use to him, Martha had been expecting (or hoping) to enter menopause, even though she was only thirty-five years old.[10] Instead, her suspected menopause turned out to be her last child, Anna. Nevertheless, apparently Martha did have a very premature menopause soon thereafter.

Freud was not, in fact, someone who particularly cared for sexuality. It was, in his view, a "compulsion."[11] Certainly from today's perspective Freud was on the prudish side. He obviously found his early discoveries about child-

---

* The idea was to overcome the death instinct by mobilizing the life instinct.

hood sexuality repellent, and he always had more than a touch of the puritan in him. He sent his sons, for example, to another doctor to inform them about the facts of life.[12]

Despite the fact that in his writings he was tolerant of masturbation, listing its helpful as well as harmful aspects, when one of his adolescent sons came to him with worries about masturbation, Freud responded by warning the boy very much against it.[13] An estrangement between father and son ensued. While Freud did not consider masturbation a vice, it was nonetheless a "symptom." Freud was never able to quite detach himself from shame over sex, and his outward war against Victorian moralism reflected a struggle within his own soul.*

Although puritanical by temperament, on some occasions Freud could close his eyes to misdoing. One of Freud's sons became an accomplished Don Juan, and picked a patient of his father's to have an affair with while she was in analysis; the conditions of analytic treatment would insure that Freud knew of the affair and very likely of the details as well. As a father Freud had been on the whole tender, but remote and perhaps neglectful of his sons. He was early on discontented with the three of them, since none had the talent to carry on his genius; perhaps this also explains why Freud needed to make surrogate sons of his pupils. For a real son to keep an aged father so informed of his sexual exploits may well have constituted a kind of revenge.

---

* The early analysts were often almost laughably austere about sexual pleasure. James J. Putnam, for example, fixed the seat on his daughter's bicycle lest she be unduly stimulated.[14]

Although Freud did so much to elucidate the early stages of child development, based not on the direct observation of children but on reconstructing the pasts of adult patients, he was not a man to turn to for advice on child-rearing. While a great theorist about the development of the small child into adulthood, he could be curiously narrow and beside the point when it came to concrete issues. According to one of his daughters-in-law, Freud chided her greatly for cuddling her infant boy too much.[15] Since Freud was always so concerned with the psychology of the Oedipus complex, he was trying to reduce the risk of an "oedipal fixation" in his grandson. Nowadays, of course, Dr. Spock—who learned so much from psychoanalysis—would emphasize the crucial importance of the mother's demonstrative love and affection for a very small child.

Freud possessed as many contradictions as a man of his stature can be expected to have. With all his formality and elegance, he was a skilled raconteur of wonderful Jewish stories. While such a correct gentleman, he could entertain the most erratic and fanciful ideas. And whatever his own human limitations, he was capable of admiring in others what he lacked in himself. Freud always liked people of fancy and imagination. Thus Lou Andreas-Salomé was bound to represent an acquisition for him personally, as well as for psychoanalysis.

Many years later Freud wrote that he had admired Lou immensely and been very attached to her "without a trace of sexual attraction."[16] Freud was always moved by the great charm of what he called narcissistic women.[17] Through Lou Freud was in touch with the spirit of Nietzsche and the best of German cultural life. Later on Freud began to honor his favored pupils by presenting them with an antique stone to be made into a ring; although he never did this for Lou, he took her into his confidence to an extraordinary degree. In his letters of later years he discussed with her the emotional problems of his daughter Anna. For a time in the 1920's Lou became Anna's psychoanalytic therapist. Freud asked Lou to help loosen Anna's ties to him; but Lou refused. They discussed Anna together almost as if Freud's own wife did not matter at all, as if Anna were their child instead. Lou responded with all her devotion, dedicating one of her books to Anna Freud.

Freud certainly had no special fondness for women with a checkered sexual past. But in 1912 he courted Lou. Her *Journal* records him sending her flowers, and walking her home at 2:30 in the morning. These attentions are all the more noteworthy from a man who jealously husbanded his time. Lou succeeded in making Freud fall in love with her, though in a sublimated way. When she missed a lecture of his, he felt uneasy. Freud had immediately grown used to speaking for Lou. He wrote her, "I have acquired the bad habit of directing my lecture to a particular person in the audience, and yesterday I stared as if spellbound at the vacant chair reserved for you."[18]

In these pre-World War I days, before his cancer and

all the disappointments with his pupils, Freud was his most inspiring. At the height of his powers, Freud was constantly reformulating his ideas; he flourished on contacts with richly endowed human beings. Lou noticed that Freud did not care for cats or dogs. When we consider how in his old age he turned to chows for emotional sustenance, her observation suggests how much more open to human communication he was at this earlier time. He would go to cafés after scientific meetings, amplifying the issues of his lectures in discussion, ever exploring possibilities.

2   *L*ou was in an intimate position to understand Freud and his whole circle. For she had actively set out to seduce Victor Tausk, whom she ranked "the most prominently outstanding" among Freud's students.[19] Tausk was handsome, with blond hair, blue eyes, and a mustache. He was also eighteen years her junior: she was fifty-one, he thirty-three. To his friends it was strange, if not offensive, to see him involved with a woman so much older.

Lou came to Vienna flaunting her attractiveness to great men as a vehicle by which present lovers could liken themselves to the famous lovers in her past. While she was in search of talented men to identify with, Tausk could hope that being accepted as Lou's lover might help make him to psychology what Nietzsche was to philosophy and Rilke to poetry. One would think that Tausk, so enormously attractive to women, could have easily found a younger and more single-mindedly devoted woman. But Lou's very self-sufficiency, her skill in pulling out of love affairs at the opportune moment, was a special source of her attractiveness to him. Afraid of being depended upon and loved, Tausk need never feel guilty about Lou.

Lou and Tausk shared many interests in common. Tausk got her into Frankl-Hochwart's clinic in order to observe some cases. He brought her the Serbian ballads he had translated, and she accompanied him on his visits with his sons. But on Tausk's part his love for Lou ended in physical revulsion and distaste.

For the year 1912–13, however, Freud, Lou, and Tausk established a triangle which had advantages for each. Lou had recurrently had two men in her life simultaneously. She had married Friedrich Carl Andreas after he had threatened to kill himself otherwise; but she slept only with other men. Before Lou was married she had used another man against Nietzsche. (Nietzsche's sister considered her a devil.) Lou, Rilké, and Andreas traveled to Russia as a threesome. And now she had a physical relation with Tausk, alongside her deep involvement with Freud.

For Freud the arrangement had frustrations as well as satisfactions. He was jealous of Tausk's opportunity to have an affair with Lou. Tausk was much younger, more virile, and altogether a larger man physically. Freud had already acquired his scholar's stoop. When Freud stared spellbound at Lou's vacant chair, she may well have been with Tausk. On the other hand, Lou could give Freud information about Tausk. She could help keep this potentially troublesome student under control.

Meanwhile Tausk had taken Lou at least partly out of identification with Freud. Tausk was certainly glad to play the role of the great man who was currently her lover. Just as Freud was jealous of Tausk's relation to Lou, so Tausk envied what Freud could mean to her. Lou could serve as a channel from Tausk to Freud, raising Tausk's importance in Freud's eyes. For both men she was a buffer.

The Viennese psychoanalytic group was beset by competitiveness for Freud's admiration. Petty jealousies and backbiting are bound to arise in any hothouse atmosphere. To be an analyst then meant becoming a pariah in psychiatry. Having given up the quest for approval by the external world, Freud's disciples needed his favor in exchange. He provided the inspiration, and, more mundanely, the patients. These apostles gave all their devotion to Freud and turned their hostilities onto the outside world. His believers followed whatever Freud was then working on, without daring to stray very far from the legitimate borders that he defined. The Society had an air of secrecy. Political or religious imagery can best convey the atmosphere of those early meetings. As Tausk put it, "Darwinism . . . was a scientific religion just as psychoanalysis is."[20] If Freud reigned as God, it was his students who made his word law.

Freud, to be sure, encouraged the absolute devotion of his students. Hated and maligned, he was entitled to entice followers by exaggerating the degree to which his supporters were an embattled minority. Freud gave regular lectures before heterogeneous audiences at the university on Saturday evenings, to which his students came with spouses or lady friends; but he preferred speaking in his small group of dedicated followers. Freud was so self-critical about his ideas that he very much needed a "yes" from the outside world. Since this recognition did not yet come from the world at large, or even from Vienna's intelligentsia, approval had to come from his own little Society.

So Freud collected able people who would in effect be yes-men. They were the audience for which he wrote. He wanted them to mirror back his ideas, to help him see his concepts in a slightly differently light. But he did not want to be jolted out of a line of thinking already embarked upon. Even if original ideas were brought by others as a sign of their positive relation to Freud, these might seem to him like a hostile attack. "What he wanted was to look into a kaleidoscope lined with mirrors that would multiply the images he introduced into it."*[21]

As a woman, Lou would arouse none of Freud's feelings

---

* In the 1920's Freud was enchanted by a paper of one of his students. As he said approvingly, "I feel as if a painter has done my portrait, and when I look at it, it is better than the original." The paper had systematized some of Freud's concepts, without suggesting any new formulations.[22]

of rivalry. For such an old-fashioned man women simply did not exist as competitors. He wanted corroborators rather than collaborators, and Lou fit perfectly into such a passive role. She could flatter him while believing everything she said. And as a woman she could take a special delight in pleasing this man. A woman can more easily dissociate her sense of self from her professional work, so to give Freud what he wanted in no way compromised her integrity.

Freud's demand that his students identify with him would eventually mobilize rebellion in men. For a man really to be like Freud meant finally for him to be original. Yet originality ended his usefulness to Freud. On the other hand, for a woman like Lou to reflect Freud's ideas back to him fitted in perfectly with her feminine ability to identify with creative men. But for one man to flatter another can be corrupting, and the best of Freud's male pupils left because the atmosphere was too narrow and ultimately degrading.

Some have likened Freud and his circle to a reigning monarch with a court, an obvious comparison for those who lived under the Hapsburg monarchy. Freud certainly had this much significance for them all. His pupils were his subjects, owing fealty to him alone; they performed tasks, wrote articles, expounded his ideas. Yet often Freud did not respect them because they lacked independence. Another image which has been used by analysts who lived through those days is that of the large extended family, with Freud as the unquestioned head. In these terms Freud needed his pupils as adopted sons, to escape isolation and to establish his immortality. Both images imply that if the pupil were not respectful toward the leader and his ideas, he would be in danger of being ousted. Very often the followers were more stringent than Freud in interpreting the permissible range of thinking.

Lou captured this whole atmosphere in one tiny vignette in her diary; her involuted sentences repay the closest attention. Early in her stay she reported a meeting at which Freud tried to counter Jung's influence on psychoanalytic thinking. Freud argued that Jung's term "complex" was unnecessary. ("Complexes" then referred to what we now call "emotional conflicts.") According to Lou, Freud

showed a subtle and ingenious bit of malice in his attempt to make the term "complex" superfluous, pointing out how it had insinuated itself into the terminology out of convenience, without having grown up on psychoanalytic soil, just as Dionysus was artificially exalted from being an exotic god to becoming the son of Zeus. (At this, Tausk, who was sitting or standing next to Freud, and was still in the white doctor's smock he wore coming from the psychiatric clinic, did not quite stifle a chuckle.)[23]

Both Lou and Tausk obviously understood the undercurrents of Freud's comment. He was likening himself to an immortal god capable of conferring divine favors or withdrawing them from an artificially created son.

If Jung were not to be Freud's successor, then Tausk might yearn for recognition. Even if Tausk did not expect to be accepted quite yet as Freud's most beloved son, he might well have seen himself as the future recipient of royal favors once the defecting barons were driven out. Supporting Freud in his quarrel with Adler, Tausk displayed a degree of malice that Lou considered excessive and unfair. And at the height of Freud's public battle with Jung, Tausk thundered against Jung's heresy. "Clever and dangerous," Lou reports Freud saying about Tausk, "he can bark and bite."[24] Tausk had indeed an aggressive mouth; his beautiful teeth were a prominent part of his face, especially when he smiled. And in these verbal battles Tausk was at his best, though in his articles too he could be truculent and polemical. As Freud commented in his obituary praising Tausk, "his passionate temperament found expression in sharp, and sometimes too sharp, criticisms...."

In listening to Tausk lecture on psychoanalysis, Lou had the impression "not only of classical Freudian theory but also of an unusually loving and reverent approach to the essential discoveries of Freud...." She objected only that Tausk was "*too* precisely Freudian; in any case, he is never likely to be reproached with the contrary."[25] Lou felt that for Tausk's own good his identification with Freud should not descend to imitation. The first to give lectures on psychoanalysis for the lay public, Tausk could repeat Freud word for word. Freud himself was a great orator. But the more Tausk felt impelled to ape Freud, the less of a personality in his own right he became.

3 *L*ou saw with the lightest possible touch just exactly the sources of tension between these two men. The human spirit can be irrepressible, for Tausk had been in Freud's circle for only a few short years before he had become a rival in Freud's eyes. Ellen Delp, a woman who was an intimate friend of Lou's, looked on Tausk as "a genius of Freud's own stature bearing up loyally under Freud's jealous provocation."[26]

What put Freud off? Lou reported that in a discussion after one of Tausk's papers, "Freud's rejoinders were more severe than usual and yet no other person presents his papers to him with such evident reverence. I think that Tausk is of all the most unconditionally devoted to Freud. . . ."[27]

In a few areas Tausk was forging ahead of Freud. For example, he wanted to extend psychoanalytic thinking to the psychology of the artist. He delivered an early paper on sublimation, focusing on the role of inhibitions in artistic creativity. This would one day be considered a perfectly legitimate subject among analysts, but in 1912 Freud felt that "with the persistent calumny of our whole movement on the part of official science, we should not dare to move so boldly into new territory leaving the rear so exposed, and confirmation of earlier discoveries needs to be made again and again." After this meeting Lou noted Freud's conflict with "independent, or temperamental, characters."[28]

Freud characteristically wished to transcend all previous limits of knowledge. Yet when it came to Tausk, Freud thought he was seizing problems ahead of their time. In his obituary, Freud noted Tausk's gift for exploring the philosophic implications of psychoanalysis. Once again, though, Freud hesitated. "Perhaps the time was not yet ripe for laying such general foundations as these for the young science of psychoanalysis." Tausk, according to Freud, had an "impetuous urge for investigation."

When Freud was submerged in following a theme of his own, he would push aside anything that interfered with it. As his earliest biographer noted, "he finds it a nuisance when lights other than his own are thrown athwart his path, or when others try to push him forward or to divert him from his chosen course. Whenever necessary he erects outworks to cut off inconvenient cross-lights."[29] Tausk's interests were disturbances to Freud. Tausk pursued fields where Freud thought the way would be blocked, and under those circumstances Freud soon lost interest.

In contrast to Tausk's universalistic aspirations, Freud believed in the single-minded pursuit of research. The only way to make important discoveries, he thought, was to "have one's ideas exclusively focused on one central interest."[30] In part Freud was reacting to the diversity of his own youth. He recorded how in "complete contrast to the diffuse character of my studies during my earlier years at the University, I . . . [developed] an inclination to concentrate my work on a single subject. . . ."[31] Freud admitted his contribution to psychology was one-sided: he claimed only to have unearthed the importance of unconscious motivation, other motives being commonplace. Defending his own narrowness, Freud thought that he "must have needed this one-sidedness in order to see what remains hidden from others."[*][32]

Tausk's work irritated Freud, and a good part of the problem was Tausk's originality. Lou and Freud talked it out repeatedly, while she was still engaged in her affair with Tausk. In her diary Lou mentioned having supper at Freud's: "earlier in the living room he turned the conversation to Tausk and we talked a lot about him; the same later in his study and it was nearly half past one when he took me home."[33] On another evening Lou wrote that "before supper, and then again later, Freud talked readily and at length about the Tausk problem. At the end he spoke kindly and tenderly."[34] Evidently this spiritual *ménage-à-trois* arrangement was accepted quite naturally by them all.

Tausk's independence disturbed Freud. He recognized brilliance, admired creativity, but in his immediate circle he needed passive receptacles for his concepts. At this stage Freud was still trying to keep his best students. He hoped to reconcile psychoanalysis's need for first-rate adherents with his own manner of working out his ideas. But

[*] For an amplification of the uses of such one-sidedness, cf. my *Freud: Political and Social Thought*, pp. 76–90.

Tausk's talents upset Freud's inner harmony. Lou reported after one of the Society's meetings that

Freud acts with complete conviction when he proceeds so sharply against Tausk. But . . . bearing in mind Tausk's original neurotic disposition . . . it is also clear that any independence around Freud, especially when it is marked by aggression and display of temperament, worries him and wounds him quite automatically in his noble egoism as investigator, forcing him to premature discussion. . . .[35]

Freud resented Tausk's intellectual ambitiousness, preferring men like Otto Rank who, according to Lou, was at that time "a son and nothing but a son." Of Rank Freud said to Lou, "Why is it that there can't be six such charming men in our group instead of only one?" As Lou shrewdly noted, in Freud's wish for half-a-dozen Ranks "the individuality of the man referred to is put in some doubt."[36]

The crux of "the Tausk problem" was not just that Victor was a son striving to grow up; for Tausk's independence was partly a façade. His inhibitions in being fully creative made the situation with Freud acute. For worst of all, from Freud's point of view, was that at times Tausk stayed glued to Freud's own preoccupations. In an uncanny way Tausk seemed able to anticipate Freud's own formulations. Hence Lou's reference to Tausk's forcing Freud to "premature discussion." Freud felt uneasy with Tausk not just because he had a mind of his own, but also because he dared to use this talent on problems which mattered so very dearly to Freud himself. One passage of Lou's conveys Freud's distress:

In the afternoon after Tausk had finished the lecture . . . we drove to the meeting. I went on ahead and walked with Freud, who was waiting for me in the street. He was restless (on account of the closeness of the ideas to his own), questioned me during the lecture, passing a note to me: "Does he know all about it already?"[37]

Here lay the center of Freud's difficulties with Tausk; and Freud's distress that Tausk might steal some of his ideas before he had quite finished with them also helps explain why Lou could be useful to Freud in keeping an eye on Tausk. Freud could be sure on whose side she would ultimately come down. He felt uncomfortable with someone like Tausk around, a man bright enough even to anticipate some of his own concepts. Freud did not like the uncertainty lest Tausk have an idea before he did. And it bothered Freud to have to acknowledge Tausk's contributions. Again in Lou's diary we can find a subtle reference to Freud's awareness of his problem in relation to Tausk. Tausk had made a comment early in a meeting, and "at the close of the discussion Freud referred favorably to this clarifying observation—having immediately forgotten who had made it. He then smilingly apologized for his error."[38]

Freud could smile at Tausk's suggestions getting underfoot and at his own unwillingness to give Tausk due credit.

The situation never got beyond Freud's control. Ultimately Freud could afford to brush Tausk aside completely. But for Tausk the whole conflict touched close to the center of his being. Lou was sensitive enough to see it all from the perspective of Tausk's inner difficulties.

Only now do I perceive the whole tragedy of Tausk's relation with Freud: that is, I realize now that he will always tackle the same problems, the same attempts at solution, that Freud is engaged in. This is no accident, but signifies his "making himself a son" as violently as he "hates the father for it." As if by a thought-transference he will always be busy with the same thing as Freud, never taking one step aside to make room for himself. That *seemed* to depend so much on the situation, but ultimately it is his own doing.[39]

Lou knew enough about Tausk to understand how much he was one of those psychoanalysts who "stand themselves in practical need of the method they profess."[40] However, she greatly exaggerated the degree to which Tausk could only follow along in Freud's footsteps; for at this time Tausk was already making thoroughly original contributions by pioneering the application of psychoanalytic insights to the understanding of psychoses. (Freud held himself at some distance from psychotic clinical problems, restricting his work to the less severely disturbed, to neurotics.) Lou was right, however, that Tausk was self-absorbed and introspective, excessively ambitious and yet passionately loyal to Freud. The situation was in fact such that Tausk could place all the blame on Freud for their mutual difficulties. Lou saw too the difficult circumstances under which Tausk labored—his need to prepare for his medical examinations along with his responsibilities toward his sons.

Lou recognized the extent to which Tausk's troubles came from within his own discordant soul. "What he wants is his blind and dumb self-expression alone, suffering so greatly as he does under the burden of himself." Tausk clung to Freud partly because of his own lack of inner resources. No matter how brilliant and independent he might be, somewhere he did have a "gap in creativity," which got "filled by identification with the other (son-ship) which constantly begets the illusion of having attained the anticipated position." Tausk could be profound in his psychological understanding of others as a displacement of "his own longing to be analyzed himself,"[41] and so at times be as self-deceptive as anyone.

Lou loved in Tausk his helplessness before his inner being, his tortured struggle to use his intellect to master his passions. He was demanding, but his capacity to have illusions made him lovable. His self, however, remained the prisoner of the past. In Tausk, she wrote,

there still remain those irreconcilable contradictions between that which Freud calls the "beast of prey" (which at least helps him in the practical management of life) and his own oversensitivity to the point of self-dissolution. It is all so painful to behold that one would like to look the other way and run away. He is deceiving himself about me with his fantasies. In the long run no helpful relationship is possible; there can be none when reality is cluttered by the wraiths of unabreacted primal reminiscences. An impure tone resonates through everything, buzzing as it were with murmurings from within.

Yet from the very beginning I realized it was this very struggle in Tausk that most deeply moved me—the struggle of the human creature. Brother-animal. You.[42]

CHAPTER III

Plagiarism

1   *F*or good or ill, the outside world never leaves us entirely alone with ourselves. In June 1914 Tausk completed his medical studies. His new life had finally started. As Freud later put it in his obituary, Tausk "had begun building up a considerable practice and had achieved some excellent results. These activities promised the rising young doctor full satisfaction as well as means of support; but he was all at once violently torn from them by the war." With the First World War everything collapsed around Tausk again. Patients grew scarce and the practice of psychoanalysis became almost impossible. Freud's group met less frequently as its members scattered. Just before being called up for the army in August 1915, Tausk assembled a collection of his poems, a number of which had already appeared in print in various journals; but the collection as a whole was never published.

Tausk's children had already been sent away to a boarding school in Bohemia. Martha had found it increasingly hard to bear the responsibility for their education, and when her father died in the midst of the upheavals of the war it was not easy for her to find another job. In Zagreb Victor's mother took pity on Martha's plight, and invited her to come where food would be easier to get. In September 1915, Victor's father fell ill of a stroke. Victor had no money for a leave. As he wrote to Martha at the time, "I feel not equal to the misery at home because I am keeping my own psychical existence by mobilizing my last forces. I cannot help others. I am allowing this horse-cart of fate to run over me. We shall see with what a skeleton I shall start the new life after the war for the n-th time."*

By December 1915 he was stationed as an army psychiatrist in Lublin, which was then part of Russia although occupied by Austrian troops. Here he could take a few private patients in addition to his army work. He also found time to write. Despite how wretched he makes himself sound in letters to Martha, he possessed the inward resources to produce his best psychoanalytic writings during this trying war period. The next spring, on March 25, 1916, his father died. "Peace to this much tested man," Tausk telegraphed home. His work schedule kept him tied down from morning to night. As he wrote to Martha later that same spring, "Work from 8:00 in the morning till 7:00 at night to complete exhaustion."†

* September 30, 1915.
† May 13, 1916.

Throughout his adult life Tausk had been able to rise above social conventions. During war service he acted with genuine heroism in protecting deserters from the Imperial Austrian Army. The war enrolled peasants who had never understood what conscription meant. Helpless and confused young men found themselves in danger of being shot for their simple primitive desire to creep back to the shelter of their homes. Tausk wrote an eloquent article on the psychology of deserters,[1] which stands today as one of the earliest applications of psychoanalytic findings to law. Repeatedly he endangered himself by his kindness and unselfishness in behalf of these men. He also must have relished the opportunity, it should be added, to act in defiance of his superiors.

Tausk went out of his way to save people, using psychiatric diagnoses for humane ends. Tausk had a brusque manner, but he could act on his human tenderness. He intervened, for example, in behalf of a young boy who was to be court-martialed for failing to help shoot a whole group of enemy prisoners. Tausk saved his life by testifying that such a boy, raised with the highest standards of civilized life, could not be expected to assist in such an execution. (Years later Tausk's younger son met this man, Fritz Weiss, in South America. He had Tausk's photograph on his wall, and was full of gratitude.) Perhaps it was this sort of bravery that Freud referred to in Tausk's obituary: it was "greatly to his honor that during the war he threw himself wholeheartedly, and with complete disregard of the consequences, into exposing the numerous abuses which so many doctors unfortunately tolerated in silence or for which they even shared the responsibility."

Tausk's few private patients, however, soon drifted away. The old problem of helping his family continued to plague him. In December 1916 the army transferred him from Lublin to Belgrade, in the Serbian theater. Early in 1917 his sons got themselves expelled from school. (Hugo had indulged in a youthful escapade, whereas Marius had run into trouble with the Catholic father who taught religion by somewhat rudely repeating what he had heard from a Lutheran teacher concerning financial troubles which the Archbishop of Mainz had had in the fifteenth century.) In 1918 the Austrians were so confident of their military position in Serbia that they allowed officers to have their families with them. So in the summer of 1918 Tausk's two sons joined him in Belgrade.

Throughout the war Tausk managed to visit Vienna occasionally, often to discuss one of his new papers. He presented an important paper on war psychoses to the Vienna Society, and one on the "influencing machine" in schizophrenia—which by itself has established his psychiatric reputation. His relationship to Freud seems to have stabilized at its prewar level. Freud had to admire Tausk's work. His military service had not interfered with his growing scientific productivity. In the shrunken Vienna psychoanalytic group of the war years, Tausk loomed even larger for the future of Freud's movement. As Freud said in his obituary, Tausk's "numerous contributions . . . were distinguished by sharp observation, sound judgment and a particular clearness of expression." Clarity was always Freud's highest praise.

On the other hand, Tausk's work continued to come dangerously close to Freud's own. Freud was also hard at work during these years, outlining new concepts that touched on the problem of psychosis. In private Freud could be quite devastating about Tausk's thinking. Freud wrote to Lou, for example, on January 31, 1915: "I know that your concern with Tausk's work helped familiarize you with the subject of narcissism. But his constructions were totally unintelligible to me."[2]

Toward the end of the war Freud found unexpected sources of support. The First World War (as later the Second) stimulated psychiatric interest in psychoanalytic concepts. Emotional problems interfering with a soldier's duties, the "war neuroses," became a troublesome issue for the military authorities. Encouraged by the city of Budapest, psychoanalysts met there on September 28 and 29, 1918, for their first international meeting since 1913. The Budapest Congress marked a turning point for psychoanalysis, and everyone felt it at the time. The city officials welcomed the analysts, and Freud now won the support of a very wealthy Hungarian family.

Tausk came from Belgrade and delivered a paper on "Psychoanalysis and the Capacity for Judgment." He fell ill during the proceedings of the Congress, however, and vomited; his sickness created quite a stir at the time. But no one now knows what might have ailed him then. In his obituary Freud mentioned that at Budapest Tausk, "who had long been suffering from physical ill health, was already showing signs of unusual nervous irritability."

At these meetings in Budapest Dr. Herman Nunberg first proposed that all future psychoanalysts be required to undergo an analysis themselves. We must keep in mind that in those far-off days nothing like formal training in psychoanalysis existed; all the institutes and seminars of our own day had yet to be set up. The personal analyses of candidates in psychoanalytic training have now come to be the center of their work. But prior to Nunberg's suggestion fifty years ago, Freud had only hinted in his writings that the emotional problems of an analyst might interfere with the progress of his patients. Although in his extreme old age he once recommended that analysts undergo an analysis every five years, in these earlier times he had merely mentioned the advantages to a therapist of an analytic "purification."[3] Only to the very young candidates who came to him for advice would he suggest that they be analyzed themselves.

For the generation that had come to Freud before the war, the notion of a "didactic" analysis for teaching purposes seemed much less attractive. Although it may ultimately be hard to distinguish between a therapeutic and a training analysis, in theory the former aims to relieve psychological suffering while the latter seeks to prepare the patient for the practice of the profession. Freud might sometime talk as if patients were neurotic and analysts "normal," but he certainly did not act that way. Nunberg's suggestion implied that analysts too had emotional blocks which could be alleviated through therapy.

But Nunberg's proposal also meant that the group's more informal methods of learning, talking with Freud and with each other, had been an inadequate preparation for the practice of psychoanalysis. Nunberg, four years younger than Tausk, had recently undergone a brief therapeutic relationship with one of Tausk's contemporaries, Paul Federn. Who, however, would be available to analyze Tausk or Federn? Only Freud would have the appropriate seniority. Yet Freud as their analyst would only complicate already hyperinvolved ties. Going to Freud for an analysis meant even more of a submission than these men had already made to him. For the younger generation, and for the new recruits who would be even more distant from Freud, a personal analysis might be more feasible.

Nunberg would not have proposed making a didactic analysis a formal requirement without being sure beforehand that Freud was favorably inclined to the notion himself. It was an obvious hope of Freud's for the future. Nunberg was not then the senior figure he became in later years. His sourness did not suit him temperamentally to be a favorite of Freud's. While far enough along in his career to make such an important proposal at a public meeting, he lacked sufficient standing to ensure its passage. It was not humiliating, in other words, for him to be voted down. His motion was rejected, as he explained many years later, "because Rank and Tausk energetically opposed it."*4

Otto Rank, like Tausk a member of that early group who could not conceive of going to any analyst but the master, may have felt reluctant to involve himself with Freud any further. Moreover, a personal analysis was partly superfluous to those who had known Freud's work so intimately. Already so devoted to the cause, they needed no trial period, no "novitiate."5 Rank, however, is already well known in intellectual history. Nunberg's remembering Tausk's opposition to the motion, and his coupling the name with Rank's, is an additional indication of the weight given to Tausk's views. To Nunberg Tausk was a great figure.

For his service in the army Tausk had risen to the rank roughly equivalent to a U.S. first lieutenant (*Oberarzt*). According to his obituary, Tausk received "official commendation." Not long after the Budapest Congress, and soon after his boys had been permitted to join him, the front in Yugoslavia abruptly collapsed. The officers fled lest they become prisoners of war. Tausk returned to Vienna on the evening of November 4, 1918, and immediately tried to resume his psychoanalytic practice.

* In 1925 at the Congress in Bad Homburg this rule was finally adopted.

2   *V*ienna, however, was in economic chaos. The Empire of the Hapsburgs had been stripped away, and the city, no longer the great center of old, was almost deserted, a shrunken remnant of its former self. Getting food became a problem. The Freuds, for example, were supplied by followers and patients. Others tried to rely on friends in the country. It was a struggle to get coal for heat. The Freud apartment was even colder than others, since for the sake of their privacy they chose to live in their own separate rooms rather than in a few central ones.[6] The winters of 1918–19 and 1919–20 were the most difficult. In addition to everything else, the value of money began to disappear as inflation set in. Prices rose faster than Freud's fees and he lived off capital. When the inflation stopped his lifetime's savings had been practically wiped out.

It was not an easy time for anyone in Vienna, and particularly for those without an established profession. Tausk's situation was especially acute, and he might well have been discouraged. Almost forty, he still had to live like an impoverished student, while trying to help support a family.

As a psychoanalyst Tausk was left peculiarly exposed to these difficult conditions. In those days an analyst did not practice a little psychotherapy, with a few sessions over a short time span, in addition to full-scale psychoanalyses. (An analysis then meant six sessions a week on a couch for approximately six months or a year.) Nowadays, in contrast, psychoanalysts regularly use their skills outside strict psychoanalytic treatment. But being a pupil of Freud's in that era meant practicing psychoanalysis in all one's psychotherapeutic time. In fact, even as late as 1938, for a candidate in the Vienna Psychoanalytic Society to practice psychotherapy on the side would have been considered an interference in his psychoanalytic training. As long as Freud lived he felt he had not triumphed, so he demanded his followers' total devotion to psychoanalysis.

Any patient in search of short-term psychological support would have been unlikely then to have turned to a Freudian. And in such a disorganized social situation, few patients were in a position to undergo formal psychoanalysis. Although an analysis was then a considerably less lengthy treatment than today, it still required a minimum degree of economic and political security. Furthermore, all analytic patients had to come to an analyst via Freud. Tausk had left himself dependent on Freud's personal favor and acceptance. In addition, if patients were not American they probably would be unable to pay. And even if they paid, the currency might be worthless in the near future.

Many of Tausk's friends and associates shared these problems. Yet most of them did not find themselves in as vulnerable a position. Paul Federn, for example, had come to psychoanalysis from internal medicine. So in this crisis he could easily fall back on his strictly medical practice.

Since hospital positions paid poorly, Tausk began to

search for an academic post in psychiatry, even though he had the greatest contempt for the field. Viennese psychiatry was highly descriptive and formalistic, still lacking the dynamic understanding of inner conflicts that Freud's method had made possible. Yet Tausk shared Freud's own ambivalence toward psychiatry, and while he held it in low esteem, he cared very much about a university position.

On the basis of his wartime writings on psychotic problems, Tausk could justifiably feel entitled to such an appointment. Freud wrote in Tausk's obituary that "his clinical activities, to which we owe valuable researches into various psychoses (e.g., melancholia and schizophrenia), justified the fairest hopes and gave him the prospective appointment to a University Lectureship [*Dozentur*] for which he had applied." A psychiatric post was waiting for Tausk any time he wanted it in Belgrade or Zagreb. Just having re-experienced life in a backward country, however, he was not ready to renounce his ambitions for a career in Vienna. To become a *Dozent* at the University of Vienna would have been the making of his career. Perhaps Wagner-Jauregg had promised it to him. But to aim to be a *Dozent* while remaining affiliated with Freud meant difficulties. Being a psychoanalyst was no asset in the university circles of that time.

Simultaneously Tausk had one other, and in a sense, contradictory, aspiration which his productivity in writing articles during the war also encouraged him in. Within a month or so of returning to Vienna Tausk went to Freud to request an analysis. Tausk's great dream now was to be analyzed by Freud. Whatever the opinions of the academics, Freud was the greatest psychologist of his time. Tausk had enough substantial work behind him to feel entitled to this privilege, and he had just embarked on writing a psychiatric book. He knew full well that he still had unresolved personal problems, and it would have been inconceivable for him to have gone to any analyst other than Freud.

Tausk had just recently opposed Nunberg's motion that a training analysis be made mandatory for all future analysts. Tausk's stand on the issue might have represented his anxiety lest Freud not take him into analysis. For while Tausk recognized that his own inner difficulties persisted, he must have known that his presence caused Freud discomfort. Lou had seen as early as the Munich Congress in 1913 that Freud "plainly held him off."[7] Disagreeing with Tausk's formulations on narcissism, Freud found them incomprehensible. Yet Freud had spoken well of Tausk's most recent work on schizophrenia.[8] Freud may have harbored old jealousies because of Lou, but the erotic tie between Tausk and Lou had been over for five years now. To the external world Tausk at this point had nothing, and he came back from the war needing help.

Freud's answer was no. The implications of Freud's refusal no doubt took some time to sink in, but the brute fact was not concealed at the time. Tausk spoke of it to his sister Jelka in Vienna, and Freud later defended this refusal to his other pupils. Freud explained to Nunberg, for example, that he had rejected Tausk because he was a "dog on a leash." Freud feared that if he took Tausk into analysis, the "problem" at the Society would worsen and there would be an open quarrel between them. Freud was afraid, as he put it to Nunberg, that Tausk would "bark" at him; Tausk threatened to eat Freud up.[9] Although this refusal further strained his relationship to Tausk, Freud still thought he could hold him within the fold. He referred a patient to Tausk on December 7, 1918, but one who could not afford to pay for treatment.

Freud tried to work out a compromise with Tausk. He recommended that he go into analysis with a psychiatrist more than five years Tausk's junior, Dr. Helene Deutsch, whom Freud himself had taken into analysis earlier that fall. She had been with Freud for about three months when Tausk began to go to her for treatment in January 1919. Tausk was, in fact, her first psychoanalytic case, although she already had considerable psychiatric experience. Her decision to come to Freud represented an acquisition for Freud's group in Vienna.

She had made her arrangements to be analyzed by Freud in the spring of 1918. When she first broached the subject to Freud, he had asked what she would do if he sent her to someone else. She replied that she would not go into analysis with anyone else, and so he agreed to take her in the fall of 1918. As a woman, Helene Deutsch already stood out. Only seven women had been in her class at medical school; only three finally received their degrees. And few female physicians were practicing psychiatry in those days. Although in later years psychoanalysis was to become a field in which women were able to advance to the top of the profession, at that time Freud had accepted very few for training. When Freud accepted Dr. Rado-Révész, a female psychiatrist from Hungary, Helene Deutsch was encouraged to believe that he might take her too. In fact she replaced Dr. Révész as a patient, taking her analytic hour.

Helene Deutsch was not entirely a newcomer to Freud's circle in the fall of 1918 when she began her analysis with him. While normally one had to get Freud's special permission to join the heterogeneous audience at his lectures, as a member of Wagner-Jauregg's staff at the clinic she (like Tausk) was automatically eligible to come. At least as early as 1914–15 she heard Freud lecture in Wagner-Jauregg's auditorium. She had first learned about Freud's ideas while a student in Munich, where she had gone for a year (1911) to study schizophrenia under the famed Emil Kraepelin. (Kraepelin brought a great deal of system to psychiatry, and modern psychiatrists still work with his distinctions in mind; Freud, however, thought of him only as a "coarse fellow.") While she was in Munich a friend of hers in Vienna, Dr. Joseph Reinhold, sent her a copy of Freud's *Interpretation of Dreams*. At the time she was working with a confused schizophrenic. When she used Freud's concepts to help understand this patient, a nurse wondered which of them was the crazier. But for the first time Helene Deutsch felt she could comprehend her patient's conflicts.

When she returned to Vienna she heard more and more about Freud's work. In 1916 she was invited by Freud to comment on a very difficult paper by Lou Andreas-Salomé at the Vienna Psychoanalytic Society.* Gradually Helene's name creeps more and more into the proceedings of the group. By 1918 she had begun to give her own presentations there. At an evening devoted to Tausk's paper on the "influencing machine" in schizophrenia (January 18, 1918), she was one of the discussants.

3 *E*ntering analysis with Freud, Helene Deutsch soon realized she would have to give up her position in Wagner-Jauregg's clinic. While she had found Kraepelin a very boring teacher, Wagner-Jauregg was a great figure in her life. Although he ridiculed her for being so interested in Freud,† he respected her as a psychiatrist. In 1913 he had urged her to return to Munich for a short time to find out what Kraepelin was doing along psychological lines.

* One can only wonder if Freud perceived any similarities between Lou and Helene. Certainly Helene thought of Lou as a rival successful woman.

† For example, he might say to a patient of hers: "Has Dr. Deutsch put in your mind that you want a child from your father?"

Wagner-Jauregg's clinic was, to repeat, the stronghold of psychiatry in Vienna; Helene Deutsch had been there for seven years, since 1912.

At that time women could not yet hold clinical positions, although they already had appointments in theoretical subjects. With the outbreak of World War I the male psychiatrists entered military service. Under these exceptional wartime cricumstances, Helene Deutsch rose to the place of assistant in charge of the women's division. Otto Pötzl was the assistant in charge of the men's section. (He later became professor of psychiatry in Prague and finally came back to Vienna as Wagner-Jauregg's successor.) Although as a woman Helene Deutsch could not formally be appointed an assistant, when she later left the clinic Wagner-Jauregg gave her a letter saying she had performed the duties of this post.* Throughout the war she had the responsibility of diagnosing cases to decide whether they should be committed to asylums. In addition to these clinical tasks, she had also done some scientific writing: she published a paper on the effects of gas in damaging a portion of the human brain.

Helene Deutsch attracted Freud as a potential pupil precisely because of her involvement in Wagner-Jauregg's clinic. As with Tausk earlier, Freud was extremely flattered by every outsider who came to him. Yet when she entered analysis she realized that she would have to leave the clinic. Freud looked on official psychiatry as his enemy. The outside world had in fact reacted with hostility to Freud's

---

* In the certificate, dated November 12, 1918, Wagner-Jauregg testified that she had been "nearly" an assistant, to cover the illegality of her position.

ideas, and he turned away from it to his small group. Inevitably he felt aggressive toward anyone who had not cut his other ties. At one and the same time Freud wanted his teachings to penetrate at the clinic and yet felt that no one could serve two gods simultaneously. He was angered by his rejection at the clinic and held himself aloof from psychiatry; yet he very much wanted to change the official atmosphere.

Helene Deutsch felt that Freud's attitude toward her was either/or. Certainly others of Freud's pupils have also reported that they were obliged to secede from psychoanalysis if they had interests in other fields.[10] In her case pressure from within the clinic itself pushed her toward leaving. A good friend of hers, Dr. Paul Schilder, had come back from the war, and she knew that Wagner-Jauregg really preferred him to her. As a man, Schilder could look forward to an academic career, and in fact he eventually became a professor at Vienna. So for Schilder's sake, as well as for her ambitions with Freud, she left the clinic when she became Freud's disciple. Leaving Wagner-Jauregg, she became an assistant in Karplus's neurological clinic. Neurology, having nothing to do with psychoanalysis, would be less threatening to Freud. It was also closer to Freud's own earlier interests, since it had been his field before founding psychoanalysis.

In addition to her professional success, Helene Deutsch's personal life had been happy. In 1911 in Munich she—then Helene Rosenbach—had met an internist, Dr. Felix

Deutsch, and they were married just before she took her degree the next year. She had a baby boy late in 1917. Felix Deutsch was a *Dozent* by the time she went into analysis with Freud, so that both of them were valuable potential followers of Freud. As part of his effort to woo them both, Freud ensured their food supply by getting Felix a job on the English occupation staff. Felix Deutsch was later to become one of the founders of psychosomatic medicine.

Both Felix and Helene had known Tausk since 1911. Joseph Reinhold, one of the two witnesses at the Deutsch's wedding and the same friend who had sent Helene a copy of *The Interpretation of Dreams,* had also introduced her to his intimate friend, Victor Tausk. Like Tausk, Reinhold had changed careers to enter Freud's circle, leaving philosophy for psychoanalysis. Reinhold, however, after a time came to feel the Vienna Psychoanalytic Society was too narrow, and he escaped being stifled by gradually drifting away. (Self-preservativeness can be channeled in isolated ways, since later on Reinhold refused to recognize the Nazi menace until it was too late for him.) But in the years before World War I Reinhold was as swept up in Freud's ideas as Tausk himself. Tausk and Helene Deutsch, along with Frankl-Hochwart and Reinhold, had spent many hours together discussing professional problems. Tausk, however, had a touch of the antifeminist in him (possibly from his experience with Martha), and he could be sarcastic about Helene's career succeeding at the expense of her role as a wife. Tausk's entering into analysis with her in the winter of 1918–19 represented a very different set of roles for them both.

In the spring of 1915 Tausk's youngest sister, Nada, who was in school in Vienna, was having some difficulties with a fiancé; and Tausk, who had great affection for his sister, sent her to Helene Deutsch for treatment. She recommended that Nada break with her young man since she was not really in love with him. But Nada was not yet ready for such a step, and she stopped seeing Helene after a few sessions. It was not a formal psychoanalysis by any means. Over fifty years later Nada remembered, with some resentment, how prompt Helene Deutsch had been to dig deeply—an impulse so characteristic of Freud's pupils.

In January 1919 Freud recommended this talented psychiatrist as Tausk's analyst. Sending Tausk to her as a patient, Freud had to explain something about the case and his reasons for not taking Tausk into analysis himself. Freud told her he felt inhibited in Tausk's presence. Freud was restless and uncomfortable with Tausk, just as Lou described him earlier. And Freud did not tolerate this sort of displeasure well. Unlike later, in his extreme old age, when his daughter Anna would simply deliver papers for him at meetings, in 1919 Freud was still coming to his Society with his ideas very much in flux.

Freud told Helene Deutsch that it made an "uncanny" (*unheimlich*) impression on him to have Tausk at the Society, where he could take an idea of Freud's and develop it before Freud himself had quite finished with it.[11] Lou had noted how Freud disliked being forced into "premature discussion." The tension between the two men at the meetings of the Society would only be heightened were Freud to become Tausk's analyst.

Freud complained to Helene Deutsch that Tausk would not merely receive ideas, but would come to believe they were his alone. A struggle with Tausk over priorities, over who originated which concept first, was extremely disagreeable to Freud. The situation was essentially still what Lou had described earlier, with the added complication that Tausk had done his best work during the war, and was therefore emboldened to expect more recognition from Freud. Having Tausk in analysis would mean, as Freud explained afterward to another pupil, that he would never be able to publish another line without Tausk's thinking Freud had stolen it.[12] Tausk was the only one in the group brilliant enough to be such a rival.

The whole issue of plagiarism bothers all who write. Can anyone ever feel he has fully acknowledged all his intellectual debts? Do not students sometimes fail to acknowledge the conceptual leads of their teachers? Everyone has ideas that are latent or preformed. People might quote Freud, but not in the right places. Freud still had discoveries to make, but he might make them so convincingly that Tausk could believe he had thought of them first. Tausk could then elaborate Freud's concepts with his own clinical material, without making the distinction between what was his and what was Freud's.

Even creative writers have felt beset by this anxiety. Hemingway, for example, said that he "always had that problem—other writers pinching my stuff."[13] In science, it becomes a matter of the greatest importance who first makes a discovery. The issue of originality, and therefore of priorities, is indigenous to any scientific group. Was it Darwin or Wallace who discovered evolution through natural selection?

What is worse, the most likely channels of plagiarism are not conscious. It is quite easy to misconstrue the sources of ideas without being at all dishonest. We are all too willing to forget, literally, our intellectual obligations. Depth psychology, moreover, is a field in which very little can be objectively proven. Innovations come mainly in how we think about mental processes. In the natural sciences struggles over priorities at least concern more objective discoveries.

4   *F*reud liked to play with his ideas for years before publishing them. He often referred to having withheld the publication of a book, an essay, or even a solitary idea. After he had begun to collect students, he complained that now he had to publish too quickly.[14] In his years of isolation he could be pregnant with his ideas without outside

interferences (in his letters Freud uses images of fertilization). Freud's creativity developed in loneliness, but when the moment came for communication he needed pupils. However, when his ideas were not yet crystallized, he feared that Tausk would take them and develop them before they had stabilized in his own mind. Creativity was a digestive process for Freud, whereas with Tausk it always had to be an explosive one. A strong nucleus of reality lay behind Freud's anxieties over Tausk. Freud might well have an inner perception of an idea, long before being able to formulate it precisely.

In Tausk's presence Freud's personal manner of working was cramped. Freud was possessive about his ideas partly by necessity: there were students who did steal from him. Tausk did not just mirror back whatever Freud introduced at the Society. Lou had been perfect in that role. Tausk was clever enough to be able to assimilate Freud's ideas and develop them on his own. And it would then seem to Tausk, Freud feared, that they were all Tausk's own thoughts. So in the face of Tausk's urge for recognition, his desire to be the beloved son, not to mention his need for therapeutic help, Freud just wanted air to breathe in: he did not want someone in analysis who would argue with him. Helene Deutsch would be no such threat, since she had just come to learn.

So Freud refused Tausk. He was as honest as he could be about his reasons, and sent him to a psychiatrist he already had in analysis. The referral was flattering to Helene Deutsch but a terrible insult to Tausk. Despite her psychi-

atric experience, as an analyst Helene was a nobody. Both
she and Tausk knew that he had done much better work.
Tausk belonged to the oldest generation of analysts, few
of whom had ever been analyzed. Sending him to her only
underlined Freud's refusal of an analysis; it emphasized
that Freud was accepting other Viennese psychiatrists as
patients.*

In retrospect Freud's proposal that Tausk go into analysis
with Helene Deutsch while she was in analysis with
Freud certainly looks bizarre. But Tausk need not have
accepted the insult. Why did he go to her? At this point
Tausk's personal troubles played havoc with his career.
Lou had prophesied his inability to be fully independent.
Tausk partially recognized elements of this weakness in his
relations with women. As he could not be independent
toward Freud, so Tausk did not want others to be dependent on him. He had written to his wife that he could love
only "free" people, that those who depended on him made
him dependent, for which he revenged himself. Only by
keeping at a distance in human relationships could he
control his own sadism, and not fear the destructiveness
of his own love. Freud's self-sufficiency, therefore, like
Lou's, must have been especially attractive to Tausk. Freud
had been partially rejecting Tausk for some time; this

* Later on in that spring of 1919, Freud took into analysis someone even less
distinguished than Helene Deutsch—Dr. Robert Jokl. Freud kept Jokl only two
and a half months, explaining in advance that Jokl would be sent to someone
else as soon as Freud had a chance to decide who would be best. Freud already
had better-paying foreigners pressing for his time, and he could afford to keep
local Viennese only for a short period.

gave Tausk exactly that combination of support and distance which made him feel at ease.

So Tausk swallowed the offense, and went into analysis with Helene. Since she was herself in analysis with Freud, she could be a bridge from him to Freud. He would lie on her couch six days a week, knowing that she would be on Freud's couch just as often. Tausk could be analyzed by Freud through her. At the same time, Tausk would be re-establishing a triangular relationship with Freud through a woman. It was almost the same story as with Lou; once more an attractive woman would be the channel between the two men. Tausk knew that a woman would be far less threatening to Freud, and through her he could plead his case. To Freud, Helene Deutsch could be a source of information about Tausk, just as Lou had been.

Tausk's analysis lasted three months, from January through March 1919. Even for those days the analysis was unusually short. The analytic ideal of treatment was for the patient on a couch to free-associate, to express all his thoughts and ideas, in the presence of an analyst who would be opaque "and, like a mirror, . . . show . . . [the patient] nothing but what is shown to him [the analyst]."[15] If Freud had wanted his students to mirror back his ideas, he thought patients were entitled to the very same privilege. Freud gave to others what he wanted for himself.

The analyst should not burden the patient with any issues but only discuss those problems which the patient chooses to bring up. By the analyst's remaining cool, distant, and neutral, the patient is allowed to develop his own fantasies and expectations about the analyst. These fantasies and expectations reflect the patient's past conflicts and problems, and their projection onto the analyst constitutes the analytic "transference." The task of the analyst is then to help dissect (interpret) the transference reactions of his patient, thereby leading him to a rational understanding of his difficulties. This understanding in turn enables the patient to dissolve his emotional reactions fixed in the past.

The transference from patient to analyst was, according to this system of thought, the crucial vehicle of therapy. Yet no transference was ever established between Tausk and Helene Deutsch, or at least so it seemed on the surface. It was not simply that he knew her to be married and the mother of a small child, but that he already knew her quite well as a person—in fact, much better than he knew Freud—so it proved impossible for her to become the neutral blank screen on which he could project the emotional conflicts from his childhood. Instead of Helene's becoming a mirror for Tausk's self-understanding she constituted merely a realistic road to Freud.

In the past Tausk had clearly been disturbed. He had had periods of depression in which he was full of despair. His depressions could be agitated; for instance, at one time he used to go from movie to movie, afternoons and evenings. He was then having trouble working and reading, staying alone or being with people. But he had managed to cope with an extraordinary degree of disruption in his life. Most important, he always functioned in the demanding role of a psychiatrist, with all that means in terms of the day-to-day bearing of emotional stress.

Now, in the winter of 1918–19, he had a new set of specific problems, and in addition to everything else he was worried about his son Marius. For years Tausk had had financial difficulties; now about to turn forty, his career was as uncertain as ever. Clean and bourgeois in appearance, no one would have guessed how interesting or disturbed he could be. Physically he was getting a little flabby; he gave the impression of being round. Tausk both walked and looked now like a middle-aged man.

Whatever his inner conflicts, the economic chaos, or his strained relations with Freud, however, Tausk did seem on the way to building up some sort of practice. He was able, according to a letter he wrote Freud on March 1, 1919, to see seven patients a day, six paying and one free of charge. Tausk paid a fee to Helene Deutsch, according to the analytic rule. She thought that nothing more serious than a neurosis troubled Tausk, part of it centering on Freud. Although he was her first patient on a couch, if there had been schizophrenic elements in his problems someone with her extensive hospital training would have been expected to be able to spot them. Schizophrenia appears like a foreign body, as if the patient has something the therapist cannot quite identify with. It is true, of course, that in someone as intelligent as Tausk schizophrenia would have been very hard to see.[16]

Perhaps Helene Deutsch did not know enough to be able to diagnose Tausk's troubles. Certainly Freud had not given her any special warnings. Maybe Tausk was one of those people who are able to act a part, using a façade to live beyond their psychic means. Schizophrenia can be insidious, and Tausk may have been struggling with such a break. But any diagnosis has practical purposes; it lets one know what to expect. Never in three months of analysis was he for a moment suicidal. Tausk's relations with people were never restricted or impoverished. He was a warm and dynamic person, jolly and sociable, in good human contact. In his work he was objective and scientific. Knowing him as a living man, full of activity and love of life, no one would have guessed a melancholic past.

In his analytic sessions with Helene Deutsch Tausk talked almost entirely about Freud. Whatever Tausk's deeper difficulties, they now all centered on Freud. Tausk did not rage against Freud; he just grieved over Freud's attitude to him. Tausk thought that the trouble between them lay in Freud's own difficulties. Tausk felt that he had some ideas before Freud, but that Freud would not acknowledge them. Tausk did not directly accuse Freud of taking ideas from him, but the implication was that Freud was dependent on him. There is no doubt that Tausk was capable of having concepts of his own, which could in fact correspond to what Freud might eventually think. Outside of his being an analyst and indebted to Freud for the framework in which he thought, Tausk did not view his work as taken from Freud.

Some great men believe nothing is real unless they have thought it. Freud did not welcome the original ideas of others, because he wanted to think through everything for himself, as part of his remaking the world. Freud had a great need to arrive at any new point in his work in his own way, by the continuous development of concepts already assimilated. He could not accept the ideas of others in their original form, but first had to transpose them into his own manner of thinking.

Jones rightly treats this characteristic as Freud's defense against being "too readily influenced by others."

Freud had inherently a plastic and mobile mind, one given to the freest speculations and open to new and even highly improbable ideas. But it worked this way only on condition that the ideas came from himself; to those from outside he could be very resistant, and they had little power to change his mind.[17]

When dealing with ideas he found "foreign" to him, Freud had to work over and develop them until he managed to incorporate them within his own intellectual edifice. As he himself once wrote, "I do not find it easy to feel my way into unfamiliar trains of thought, and generally have to wait until I have found a point of contact with them by way of my own complicated paths."[18] Having pursued these complicated paths, after such a detour, would Freud himself be able to remember where he had started out? Freud's mode of thinking was bound to elicit Tausk's resentment because it prevented him from ever gaining credit for asserting himself in an original manner.

Freud's tendency to forget his sources fits his inability to understand views other than his own. As he admitted once, "it is never easy for me to follow a new train of thought that somehow does not go my own way or to which my own way has not yet led me."[19] But by the time Freud had laboriously finished making an alien idea palatable, someone else like Tausk might well think that one of his previously "unintelligible" concepts had passed silently into Freud's own hands.

While Freud was resistant to the ideas of others to the point of being able to understand them only when he could believe he had discovered them himself, he was also, as we have seen, scrupulously concerned lest others in turn claim his ideas as their own. Needless to say, in the overheated atmosphere of Freud's circle it was often very difficult to tell who had which idea first. At times Freud may have only considered an idea in his mind, but seeing it in print he would conclude that someone had stolen it. He may well have had illusory memories about what lay behind the contributions of Tausk that he felt were taken from him.*

---

* As early as 1913 Tausk had complained to his friend Edoardo Weiss that Freud was slighting his originality and hampering his work, by assimilating his discoveries into Freud's own developing intellectual system. Weiss at the time was skeptical of Tausk's complaint, on the grounds that from his own experience Tausk had something of the same trait he attributed to Freud. In

Freud's insistence on priorities inhibited Tausk's work. In his papers Tausk was scrupulously careful in citing Freud's writings, and especially in footnoting personal communications from Freud. Yet it burdened Tausk's work. At the end of one paper for example, which had been discussed at the Society, Tausk weakened the whole argument by rushing ahead to discuss some oral comments of Freud's.[20]

5   *T*he theme of plagiarism can be found almost everywhere one turns in Freud's career. Since Freud's ambition was world fame, he was bound to worry lest a discovery of his own be snatched away by someone else. For example, in the 1880's, before any of his work in psychology, Freud missed by a wide margin discovering the uses of cocaine as a local anaesthetic in eye surgery. But to Freud it seemed he had lost a great opportunity. He had wanted to visit Martha in Berlin, and so hastily finished a paper he was writing on cocaine; in his absence another Viennese physician made the great discovery. Freud wrote many years later that it had been "the fault of my fiancée that

fact, Weiss thought that a paper of his own had been prematurely beaten out by Tausk. Weiss was convinced that Tausk could confuse matters and think that he had already said this or that. So Weiss concluded that it was dangerous to reveal ideas to Tausk. On the other hand, in the 1930's Weiss had an experience of his own in which Freud forgot one of his sources, in this case a paper by Weiss.[21]

I was not already famous at that youthful age . . . but I bore . . . [her] no grudge for the interruption."[22] Like Tausk, Freud felt his talent had its costs, that his genius required great sacrifices. And, as later in his conflict with Tausk, Freud sometimes imagined that he had thought out another's achievement. For to a patient in 1909 Freud explained how he himself had really made the cocaine discovery, and deserved the honor.[23]

In 1904 Freud found himself in a quarrel over priorities that sheds additional light on the controversy with Tausk. Freud had a very intimate friendship with Wilhelm Fliess in the 1890's, and after their relationship had cooled, Freud discussed one of Fliess's pet ideas on the role of bisexuality in human life with a patient in treatment. The patient, Hermann Swoboda, in turn communicated the thought to his friend Otto Weininger, who, as Freud put it, "thereupon struck his forehead and ran home to write down his book." Weininger's book was an immense success, and Fliess demanded to know from Freud how this "burglary" of his idea had taken place.[24]

Freud tried to dodge the issue by pointing to other writers who had stressed the role of female elements in men and masculine components in women. The notion of bisexuality was at least as old as Plato. Yet as Fliess was able to make Freud remember, not only had Freud played a greater role than he wanted to acknowledge in giving away Fliess's concept, but Freud had also forgotten an early discussion with Fliess on bisexuality. In explaining his behavior Freud conceded that he had been tempted to "steal" from Fliess the "originality" of this concept.

"Ideas," Freud argued, "cannot be patented." One can only "hold them back," and one "does well to do so if one places value on priority."*[25]

We cannot be sure Tausk knew of either the cocaine or the Weininger episodes, but not long before he came to the Vienna Psychoanalytic Society a discussion had been held there in 1908 on a book by Albert Moll called *The Sexual Life of the Child*. Moll had been interested in sexual libido at least since his earlier book of 1898. Everyone in Freud's group spotted Moll as a rival, and one who did not sufficiently acknowledge Freud's own *Three Essays on Sexuality,* published in 1905. Others made similar charges, but the terms of Freud's own denunciation of Moll in the *Minutes* of the Society should be enough: Moll's study was

an inadequate, inferior, and above all dishonest book. . . . [I]nfantile sexuality was really discovered by . . . Freud; before that, no hint of it existed in the literature. . . . Moll gleaned the importance of infantile sexuality from the *Three Essays,* and then proceeded to write his book. For that reason Moll's whole book is permeated by the desire to deny Freud's influence. . . . He is a petty, malicious, narrow-minded individual.

Freud wound up by saying that it was a "great misfortune when a man who is destitute, as Moll is, of original ideas, nevertheless does have an idea for once."[27]

* Fliess induced a friend to publicly denounce Swoboda and Weininger for the "theft"; in doing so he published without permission Freud's letters on the subject. Swoboda sued Fliess for libel and for unauthorized publication of private letters. The Viennese satirist Karl Kraus took up Swoboda's cause. Swoboda, with a Viennese lawyer unversed in German libel laws and court procedures, lost the case.[26]

———

Anyone coming close to Freud's own work ran the risk of incurring his wrath. But just as often Freud simply found the ideas, as with Tausk's, incomprehensible. Pierre Janet, for example, a French neurologist, was working on the psychological significance of symptoms in the late nineteenth century. In print (1917) Freud paid him full credit, saying Janet could "claim priority of publication." However, Janet had not followed along the path Freud took, so Freud said he had "ceased to understand Janet's writings."[28] By the 1920's Janet was bluntly claiming that Freud had plagiarized his ideas and simply altered the terminology. Freud naturally resented "the libel" being "spread by French writers that I had listened to . . . [Janet's] lectures and stolen his ideas."*[29]

While Freud was competitive toward contemporaries in adjacent fields as well as brilliant students like Tausk, by World War I he also had long since begun to look at himself as a figure in the line of intellectual heroes. Psychoanalysis, by pointing out that man was subject to inner irrational forces, ranked as a great blow to mankind's self-esteem. Freud therefore compared his discovery to that of Copernicus ("though something similar had been asserted by Alexandrian science"), in that man's earth was no longer looked at as the center of the universe. Darwin too

* Freud was involved in another such controversy with William McDougall. In 1936 McDougall protested of one of his ideas that Freud "proceeds to restate it as his own, mixing it wellnigh inextricably . . . Now I am sure that Professor Freud did not mean to steal my theory; I feel sure he is not aware of having done so . . . [It was] the venial error of subconscious plagiarism."[30]

had wounded mankind's self-love by tracing its descent from the lower animals.[31] Yet Freud felt that he himself had labored peculiarly alone. Einstein, for example, "had the support of a long series of predecessors from Newton onward, while I have had to hack every step of my own way through a tangled jungle alone."[32] Jokingly Freud would say, "I invented psychoanalysis because it had no literature."[33]

And yet Freud's "isolation" was surely in part self-imposed, and indeed somewhat exaggerated. As he wrote, "I can never be certain, in view of the wide extent of my reading in early years, whether what I took for a new creation might not be an effect of cryptomnesia [hidden channels of memory]."[34] One way of coping with his own penchant for false recollections about his sources was simply to avoid reading. And so we find Freud deliberately ignoring the works of Nietzsche, a clear rival as a psychologist of the unconscious, and one who in Freud's words had more knowledge of himself "than any other man who ever lived."[35]

Freud had his own ways of protecting himself against his tendency to forget his predecessors. At times Freud would go out of his way to point out his forerunners, affirming his indifference to questions of priority and gladly accepting precursors as confirmation of his ideas, pioneers in psychoanalysis. In several of his essays and books Freud began by citing every known authority on the subject, the whole scientific literature, before going on to make his own contribution. Of course this expository technique would at the same time establish his own claims to originality.

Like Freud, Tausk craved to be recognized for the originality of his work. For his part Tausk would have also liked to have discovered all of Freud's ideas. One of the great gratifications in being a disciple of Freud's was the possibility of fancying oneself in Freud's position as the discoverer of psychoanalysis. But because of the way Freud's mind slowly enveloped alien ideas, Tausk would never be able to get credit for something new.

Freud and Tausk, then, shared a similar reproach. Part of the whole fascination of the Freud-Tausk struggle stems from their personalities being so similar. Each felt the other was taking ideas without due acknowledgment. And each had good grounds for this belief. To Freud it seemed that anything his pupils thought of was ultimately his. And to Tausk it seemed that no matter how far his mind ranged, ultimately Freud would put his own imprint on Tausk's contributions. Each was inhibited in the other's presence. Each man felt he was unique and a genius, and feared being destroyed by the other. Tausk, however, was the one who sought treatment. Having heard complaints and accusations from both sides, Helene Deutsch thought there was reality to what both felt. But in this struggle between them, it was Freud, she thought, who had taken the initiative.

CHAPTER IV

More Than a Chinese Puzzle

1   During Tausk's treatment Helene Deutsch was naturally trying to continue her own analysis with Freud. Unlike Tausk, she had come more for training than therapy. But she too paid her fee, about ten dollars an hour, which was a great sacrifice for her. In retrospect, she felt that Freud was not especially interested in her as a patient. Twice she spotted his cigar on the floor; he had been bored and dozed off, and then awakened as the cigar fell from his mouth. Yet they had such a positive relation to each other that they both just joked about it.

Objectively Helene Deutsch was a promising young psychiatrist, one of the very few women in Freud's Society. As we have seen with Lou, Freud had a penchant for a narcissistic type of woman who is very attractive to men; as a chestnut-haired beauty, Helene Deutsch filled Lou's place in this respect too. Freud went out of his way to win Helene's favor. She felt an active questing element in his behavior; and she responded with all the devotion of an adoring pupil. Her emotional transference to him was immense. Like other patients she became temporarily convinced that her analyst was in love with her. She remembers standing before a shop window after an analytic hour and musing: "But what will poor Frau Professor do?"

Food was scarce in those troubled times, and Freud's wife fell ill. So Helene regularly brought goat's milk (from two goats of hers left grazing in the garden of Wagner-Jauregg's clinic), and deposited it at Frau Professor's doorstep on the way next-door to her analytic hour.

Freud spoke much more freely with patients than analysts do nowadays. Some have said he chattered; he could be garrulous.[1] Frequently troubled by his prostate, he had to get up many times to go to the bathroom. With Helene, Freud's interpretations focused wholly on her straightforwardly oedipal relationship to her parents, her love for her father and her antagonism toward her mother. Helene read whatever analytic literature she wanted during the analysis. At this stage and with a pupil he liked, Freud was uninterested in the hocus-pocus of some later psychoanalysts who infantilize patients and mobilize magical feelings and expectations by imposing absurd restrictions on their intellectual curiosity.

In the fall of 1919, after Helene's analysis had proceeded almost a year, Freud announced rather abruptly that a patient mattering very much to him and greatly needing his help was returning to Vienna. Freud had already written up that former patient as the case history of the "Wolfman." (Even today this man thrives on being Freud's famous case.) Freud wanted to give this former patient Helene Deutsch's analytic hour.* Freud always preferred patients who had helped him make discoveries, and in his view Helene was not neurotic and needed no further analysis.

Freud concluded Helene's analysis with the explicit injunction that she stay on the road of her identification with her father. (She was her father's youngest and favorite child.) Freud thought her relationship to her father had been very beneficial for her, and at the same time he was encouraging her to remain a follower of his own, he being a surrogate for her father. Despite her objections to Freud's decision, the analysis that had begun in October 1918 ended within a year. There were, however, compensations for Helene; she could now have more personal contact with Freud, and as a matter of course he sent her more patients.

Freud's approach as an analyst at this time was to unscramble the patient's problems, give him a glimpse of his unconscious, and then let the patient work things out for himself. Whatever this limited technique failed to cure, it helped preserve a patient's independence. And the bigger Freud's turnover in pupils, the stronger his movement became.

---

* In later years the "Wolfman" came to Freud a third time for treatment, and Freud sent him to Dr. Ruth Mack Brunswick. Since the "Wolfman" had taken Helene's hour, and Ruth Brunswick was one of her rivals, Helene resented not having received this referral.

In the course of that year of analysis, Freud won himself a valuable pupil who would stay within psychoanalysis for her lifetime. Helene Deutsch quickly became one of the most prominent analysts in the movement. Being a psychoanalyst mobilized her best talents, both as a teacher and as a therapist. In addition to numerous papers, during World War II, while living in America, Helene wrote her two-volume *Psychology of Women,* which by now has gone through many printings and appeared in over a dozen countries. Her own career seems to contradict the Freudian theories of femininity which she expounds in her book. Far from being clinging and dependent, as a psychoanalytic psychiatrist she was both active and independent. Yet toward Freud and his concepts, which she did so much to make popular, Helene remained passive and receptive.

Freud was always exceptionally careful in discussing female psychology. Femininity was for him, he wrote, a riddle, an enigma. His writings are almost exclusively about male psychology; until almost the beginning of World War I the word "patient" would invariably be accompanied by the pronoun "he."[2] Yet while shy and retiring with women, Freud was for his time tolerant of their burgeoning demands for equality. For example, in his Society he had to argue against the view that women should be excluded in principle from membership. Freud implicitly idealized women; in his psychology no notion existed of a woman being either a bad mother or a bad daughter. On the other hand, Freud's most famous suggestion about women, that they basically envy the male's penis, does suggest a certain male arrogance. Freud never wrote, for example, about men envying the reproductive capacities of women. One finds in Freud's world only women who want to be men.

Freud did think that women had a "subtler understanding of unconscious mental processes."[3] But one almost gets the feeling that Freud felt he had a right to complain about the "obscurity" of women. He insisted, at various times, on their intellectual inferiority, their incapacity for sublimation, and their weak superegos.[4] He even considered women opponents of civilization, although he too shared in the discontent with its restrictions on instinctual expression.[5] Freud did not care for dependency and weakness, so he might well look down on women, who historically had been placed in a passive position.

And yet all such speculation about the bases of Freud's attitude toward women should not blind us to his capacity to get on well with them in the day-to-day course of life. His inner devaluation of femininity reflected the cultural norms of his time and did not contradict his characteristic gallantry toward women, which was entirely in keeping with his nineteenth-century good manners.

Freud had certainly known how to woo Helene Deutsch. Sending her a patient like Tausk reflected his high esteem for her talents as well as his desire to flatter her. The training of analysts was, of course, less systematized than now. If one had Freud's favor, that was all that was necessary. Helene Deutsch became a functioning member of the

Vienna Society as soon as she began her analysis with Freud. No formal system of control analyses then existed; nowadays a structured way for an inexperienced analyst to get supervision for his cases has grown up. In those days it was customary to go to Freud for advice on a case from time to time but on the whole he encouraged his disciples to use their own judgment and trust their knowledge of the case material.[6]

From the point of view of our own day, Freud looks like a very un-Freudian analyst indeed. While for propaganda purposes he advocated analyses undiluted by suggestion or educative devices, in fact Freud himself would try almost anything in an analysis once. In his writings Freud claimed that "the technique of psychoanalysis has become as definite and delicate as that of any other specialized branch of medicine,"[7] and he often compared an analysis to a surgical operation. But in practice Freud was undogmatic about matters of technique; he communicated guidelines which his experience had led him to think future analysts should follow. Above all he wanted his pupils to be good understanders.

Freud could be completely unorthodox in a way which his followers of today are scarcely aware. By and large they have adhered to his written technical instructions rather than to his living practice, which could be quite arbitrary. Freud was bold enough, for example, to analyze people living in the same house with him,* as well as

* Eva Rosenfeld, for example.

married couples,* despite his official recommendations that analysts not know patients socially and that patients not discuss their treatment. In the late 1920's Freud had five regular analytic patients, three of whom were very close relatives (one of these was in fact a favorite pupil).† Freud could also be actively interventionist with patients, as for example in advocating specific marriage choices. Occasionally he gave patients in analysis papers of his to translate, and sometimes ordered them to read his own published case histories.

Perhaps the most extraordinary illustration of Freud's allowing himself privileges he might have condemned in any other analyst was his analyzing his youngest child, Anna. Freud analyzed Anna in the period at the end of World War I. In letters Freud was quite open about this analysis, and it became a public secret to a small group of his inner circle.[8] From Freud's point of view there were probably some good reasons for doing what he did. But considering all the discussion in later years about what constitutes proper psychoanalytic technique, Freud's liberty in analyzing his own child makes one skeptical of ritualism in therapy or training.

Even for those days, however, sending Tausk to Helene Deutsch while she was with Freud looked like an unusual

---

* James and Alix Strachey, for example.

† Ruth Brunswick and her husband Mark, in addition to Mark's brother, David Brunswick.

situation. She never questioned Freud's reasons for sending Tausk to her; she simply assumed that Tausk would go to no one else. For one of the other means Freud had used to win her was to speak disrespectfully of his older pupils. Freud sometimes created trouble among his students by praising one at the expense of another. As we have seen already, he was contemptuous of that early generation of analysts who had joined him long before World War I. Out of identification with the master Helene looked down on those pupils who came to Freud when he had very little to choose from, and she assumed that Tausk, who was so superior to the others, also shared Freud's attitude.

From her point of view Tausk came as a patient in need of help. It was perfectly normal that he should come from Freud, since all the analysts relied on Freud for their cases. Freud had such confidence in Helene that later the same year he sent her a member of his own family. It certainly never crossed her mind at the time that Freud might ever have been jealous of Tausk.

Whatever Freud's motives in sending Tausk to her, or Tausk's in accepting the humiliation, the arrangement proved unworkable. Helene learned Tausk's side of his struggle with Freud. Impressed with what she considered Tausk's genius, her analytic hours with Freud became filled with talk of Tausk. Tausk therefore began to interfere with the conduct of her own analysis with Freud. Near the end of March 1919, after three months, Freud called a halt to the whole incestuous situation.

He explained to Helene that Tausk had become an interference in her own analysis, and that Tausk must have accepted her as his analyst with the intention of communicating with Freud through her. Tausk's success in fascinating her threatened the progress of her analysis with Freud. So Freud again put her in an either/or position, as when he expected her to leave Wagner-Jauregg's clinic. Freud could be like a demanding lover; he wanted all of her.

Freud made her choose between terminating Tausk's analysis with her and discontinuing her own analysis with Freud. To Helene Deutsch it did not constitute a realistic choice, but an order. With her immense positive feelings for Freud, she unhesitatingly communicated Freud's stand to Tausk. Tausk's treatment ended immediately. In those days such instantaneous terminations of analytic therapy were not as suspect as they would be now. Helene told Tausk Freud's opinion and her own decision, and that was the last she saw of Tausk as a patient. He listened and accepted, and was in no doubt from whom the rejection had really come. Although she may have implied that she could take him back when her own analysis was over, that could not soften the blow from Freud; in fact, she might well have no longer been of interest to Tausk as an analyst once she herself had finished her analysis with Freud.

Freud may have thought of sending Tausk to Helene as a compromise. It had not worked out, and he felt entitled to demand that she break it off. In those days far less was understood than today about the transference relationship between patient and analyst, as one might infer from Freud's analyzing his own daughter. It would seem quite obvious now that to send Tausk to Helene while she was with Freud would only encourage his preoccupation with Freud, as his analyst's analyst.

2   *I*n light of the prior history of Freud and Tausk, it is easy to see even more in this devilish arrangement. Freud had in a sense enticed Tausk, consciously or not, into another triangular setup, as with Lou. They could be rivals for a woman, they could use her as a bridge between them, yet this time Freud could fully control the situation. Through Helene Deutsch Freud had his revenge for Tausk's affair with Lou. Now Freud triumphed over Tausk. But before getting rid of him, Freud had wanted to find out what he had to say. Freud could not resist the satisfaction of hearing Tausk out, yet he felt safe only if he could do so at a distance.

On March 30, 1919, near the end of his analysis, Tausk wrote to Freud asking him to analyze his eldest son, Marius. Tausk included in the letter two of Marius's dreams, along with a plea that his son's fate not be the same as his own. Surely the reasons that guided Freud in refusing him, Tausk wrote, could not apply to his son.

But Freud did not heed this plea for a surrogate analysis, and Tausk must have seemed a greater nuisance than ever. Freud was through with Tausk, no matter how difficult it might prove for Tausk to accept the rejection.

Needless to say, Freud had other problems on his mind besides Tausk. In January 1919 he had founded a new private publishing house for psychoanalytic writings. Not only did his wife get severe influenzal pneumonia that spring, but also one of his influential followers in Hungary contracted cancer. And finally, the general economic and social hardship bore down on Freud as on the rest of the Viennese.

Yet his practice had revived after the war. By January 1919 Freud was treating nine or ten patients a day. On February 16 he wrote to a Swiss follower that "the general situation here is after all quite miserable, and the individual comes in for his share of it. Only the cause flourishes."[9] That spring Freud managed to compose a new essay, and to rewrite an old paper that he had had in his office for some time, "The Uncanny."

This whole period after World War I marked a turning point in the history of psychoanalysis. It was as decisive a shift in Freud's fortunes as that earlier stage when Freud emerged from his isolation and founded his school, just before Tausk entered the scene. Now, at the Budapest Congress in 1918, Freud's work had been heralded for the first time by public officials in Central Europe.

With the end of the war itself, foreign students could think of coming to Vienna to study psychoanalysis. Had

Tausk lived just one more year as an analyst, his financial difficulties would have been solved. Already Freud's correspondence revealed the extent of the pent-up demand for psychoanalytic treatment. The first foreigner after the war came from London in the autumn of 1919. By the end of 1919, the flow of foreigners had "become continuous."[10] From now on Freud was no longer a joke; he had become world famous.

Along with this success for the cause, Freud had just turned a corner in his life. According to Jones, Freud was "always obsessed with the idea that he had not long to live."[11] Based on some numerological nonsense worked out with Fliess, for years Freud had believed the superstition that he would die at sixty-one or sixty-two, in other words, in 1917 or 1918. (Many men of great talent have feared they would die too soon.) Having survived, his feelings of immortality were strengthened. With foreign currency Freud could now afford to be Zeus. Realistically, however, he could count on only a limited number of years of productive work ahead of him.

So from now on Freud was in a hurry. He would be working with a gun at his back. On several levels a chapter of his life had closed. He could not stop to bother with people who muddied his waters. Tausk wanted too much from Freud and was altogether too easily offended. Tausk had a neurotically dependent attitude toward Freud, and Freud found it easier simply to get rid of Tausk than to risk being—as Freud saw it—swallowed by him. Of course, he could well afford to dispense with an early supporter

like Tausk, now that so many fresh ones were flocking to
him from all over the world.

Tausk now tried putting his own private life in order.
The uncertainty of wartime had left little grounds for
confidence in his power to arrange his own fate. But if
he had come to a dead end with Freud, at least he might
be able to secure a measure of happiness with a woman.
No reconciliation was possible by now with Martha. She
hated psychoanalysis, his life and work; she had even
written articles against it. As far as we know he never
told her of any of his troubles with Freud.

In Belgrade near the end of the war Tausk had lived
with a beautiful young Serbian widow, Kosa Lazarević.
Tausk first met her in the street when she was in the cus-
tody of two Austrian soldiers; someone had evidently denounced her for speaking against the Austrian invaders.
Tausk had addressed her in Serbian and she protested to
him her innocence. Tausk then, as a superior officer, dismissed the soldiers and took full responsibility for Kosa's
release. In gratitude Kosa, who lived alone in a large
apartment, invited Tausk to stay with her as a protector.
As her gratitude grew into love, the affair with Victor
compromised Kosa among her people, since he was an
officer in the Imperial Army. But he so often defended
the Serbians against the authorities that in the end no one
held the liaison against her.

Kosa was generous and good-hearted, very human, and

Victor promised to marry her. However, although a member of the Serbian aristocracy, she was completely unintellectual and barely knew how to read or write. Nevertheless, she was influential and well-off, and after the war she arranged for Tausk a choice between a professorship of psychiatry at Belgrade or Zagreb. At first he preferred Belgrade, considering the Serbs better than the Croats. But once back in Vienna he realized how impossible a marriage to Kosa would be, wonderful though she had been for him in Belgrade. He had his hopes, moreover, of becoming a *Dozent* in the Austrian capital.

Whatever the rational reasons for hesitating to marry Kosa, it fitted into the pattern of his difficulties in permitting a woman to become dependent on him. It had all happened to Tausk before, and not just with Martha. In Berlin he had had an affair with Lea Rosen, who was then a dancer. She was officially cited in the court papers as one of the reasons for the divorce with Martha. Tausk had been very happily in love with Lea. In Vienna she became a very famous actress at the Burg-theater, even though she was small and Jewish, an unlikely candidate for the towering female roles then popular. In the years before the war she and Tausk often visited the home of Helene and Felix Deutsch together. Tausk had a tender and passionate relation to Lea Rosen, but he drew back at the prospect of marriage. He feared that in her admiration she would consume him. Lea was in a terrible depression after Victor broke the engagement; for some time thereafter it seemed to have crushed her life. Almost exactly the same problem arose with another woman in Tausk's life, Dr. Ilse Zimmerman. After Tausk could not go through with marriage she was completely broken down.

On one other occasion Tausk had been engaged to marry, except this time he was the one to be terribly depressed afterwards. In Lublin during the war Tausk became very disturbed because the girl he had gotten engaged to had slept with another man, and a patient of Tausk's at that. At the time Tausk expressed very pessimistic ideas about life, and because of his fiancée's betrayal felt he could no longer trust anyone.

One way or another, then, Tausk seemed singularly unsuccessful in firmly establishing a relationship with a woman. In order to speculate about the childhood sources for his difficulties we would have to know much more about his tie to his mother; Freud has taught us to look for infantile prototypes for adult love. Evidently Tausk had a selfless mother. Such a woman might well, with early overfeeding and the like, stimulate insatiable demands in her growing son. A mother can be so self-sacrificing as to immobilize her son's relations with other women. By loading him down with guilt feelings toward her, without giving him any tangible grounds for resentment, she might leave him with no alternative but to keep his distance from women in the future. There may also have been in Tausk, although this too is speculative, a deep masochistic alliance with his mother, whom he considered a victim of his father; and this may have supported his tortured relationship with Freud.

In Tausk's conscious life, much of his affection focused on his sister Jelka. It was plain to Tausk as to those who knew him that Jelka played a central role in his feelings for women. As a physical type she looked like Victor himself. She was lovely and golden-haired, combining intellectuality with feminine sexuality in a way in which Martha had failed. Jelka had been unhappily married to a doctor in Yugoslavia, but had left him and gone to Vienna. Victor encouraged her to divorce her husband, quite shocking to the family mores back in Yugoslavia.

After Victor had helped save Jelka from a terrible marriage, she fell in love with one of his friends, Ernst Gans, an Austrian philologist. Gans was a teacher of Latin and Greek, and lived with his twin brother Camillo, a tax lawyer. Jelka married Ernst and lived happily in the house with both of them. Camillo was a joyous type, counterbalancing his brother's more serious intellectuality. The household was harmonious, and Jelka received Victor there with his lady friends. She was especially fond of Ilse Zimmerman. Although Jelka was a familial love object for Victor, he did not need to flee from her. His relationship with her was tender and loving. Most of his women, though, were as dark as she was blond.

With Victor's return to Vienna at the end of the war, he realized that he could not marry Kosa and go back to Yugoslavia. With his rejection by Freud and the failure of his attempt to get analyzed, he tried to take a new woman into his life—Hilde Loewi, a concert pianist sixteen years his junior.[12] On meeting her he wrote Kosa to break his pledge. Kosa understood that now he was back in his own milieu in Vienna, and accepted his reasoning.

Perhaps the most important fact about Hilde was that Tausk had first met her as a patient who came to him for therapy. For an analyst to marry a patient was to commit the great crime of his profession. Curiously enough, few if any female analysts have ever married an ex-patient. However, there have been well-known instances the other way around, of male analysts marrying female patients.* (Perhaps this follows the same general principle governing teacher-pupil romances in general, or more broadly, the same grounds that lead men to marry women younger than themselves.) The notable cases, though, came later in the history of psychoanalysis. We can only guess how much Freud would have been offended by such marriages in 1919. He would disapprove in principle, even if it was good for the people involved, to the degree to which it damaged psychoanalysis. In the 1920's, however, he encouraged a prominent American analyst to marry a former patient.[13]

It is hard to know just how Tausk's struggle with Freud and the abrupt termination of his analysis with Helene Deutsch affected his relationship to Hilde. He did not meet her until after his analysis was interrupted. His elation at falling in love may have masked grief and mourning, and it would not be unknown for a patient to act out his emotional conflicts after such a sudden blow. Hilde may have been partly a substitute for the lost Helene.

---

* For example, Reich's first wife, Bernfeld's last wife, Rado's third wife, and one of Fenichel's wives were all former patients.

At any rate, this was one match that his sister Jelka refused to endorse. And one can see in Tausk's choice of a former patient the glimmering of his growing resentment of Freud.

Only slowly had Tausk's rebellion taken shape. Tausk's sheer geographical distance from Vienna during the war had temporarily released him from the precarious balance of his earlier relation to Freud. Far from Vienna, Tausk could be more objective about Freud; his bond to his teacher loosened and he was able to be more original and productive. But returning to the center of Freud's world Tausk re-experienced just how difficult it could be to deal with Freud while living in the same city—the more so since Tausk's wartime independence had only resulted in making him more demanding. Freud's rejection right then had been so personal that it was difficult to rationalize on any scientific grounds.

Freud had sensed Tausk's latent rivalry for years. In the very first paper that Tausk presented to the Vienna Society, he referred to Plato and Aristotle, mistakenly making the latter into the former's master. Freud picked it up immediately: "Plato is not a successor of Aristotle; he was the older man, and a student of Socrates."[14] The nucleus of rebellion lay there all along: Tausk began his relationship with Freud in competition and rivalry. (Of course, Tausk's belief that Freud needed to take his ideas may have stood all along for devaluation of his teacher.) Tausk's passionate devotion would not have been enough to make

Freud uneasy. Tausk was a fighter, as of course Freud was himself. And though Tausk was very lovable and seductive toward women, with men he could be quite sadistic. Yet Tausk mattered much less to Freud than Freud to Tausk. Contact with Freud meant more to each of his pupils than to Freud himself.

Nevertheless, Freud's response to Tausk also had its neurotic aspect. While a son may hate a father surrogate, it is equally likely for an older man to be jealous of a younger one. The Oedipus complex should not be presented only from the point of view of the son. How does a father react to murderous hate? What did Oedipus' father intend, after all, for his son? Freud was preoccupied with dying, which meant that every man could become a potential threat to him. He certainly harbored death wishes against his own sons, as he himself recorded; surely he could envy the youth of his pupils as well.[15] Freud saw in Tausk only a danger to himself, so he was therefore unable to consider that Tausk was disturbed and in need of help. Freud was much too involved to be objective.

3 *B*y 1919 a series of rebellions against Freud's authority had already broken out among his students. Adler and Jung had publicly fallen out with Freud; he referred to them as "the two heretics."[16] Unlike his success with adopted daughters, Freud had trouble with all his "sons" in psychoanalysis. Especially for men, working for such a genius could be very frustrating; it was bound to offend a man's sense of autonomy. Being close to Freud imposed a great strain on a man's tolerance of his own passivity.

Yet in a sense Freud encouraged rebellion in his students. By demanding absolute surrender from them, which they might give for a time, he mobilized their need to revolt. Freud's male pupils wanted his love, but he gave it only if they came close to castrating themselves as creative individuals. Yet at bottom Freud lacked respect for the men who became his servile followers. Although he wanted them as projective mirrors for his ideas, part of him could not admire those who handed back his ideas unchanged. He sought brilliance and independence in his students—but not too much. So in undercover ways Freud stimulated those struggles against him which disturbed so much of his working life.

By the act of rebellion, by declaring their independence, his pupils could become like Freud himself. For Freud was a great heretic, and he attracted people who shared his need for independence. Each of Freud's defecting pupils, and especially those who set up schools of their own, demonstrated in the act of defiance the depth of their allegiance to Freud.

Tausk was not content to be just one of Freud's apostles; and without a rebellion against Freud, the creative part of Tausk would have been frustrated. To the extent Tausk was a rival to Freud he was also a threat, and Freud had had some experience by 1919 in dealing with presumptuous pretenders. As he remarked about Adler and Jung, "they too wanted to be Popes."[17] At times Tausk may have imagined himself to be like Adler and Jung. Freud, however, never accepted him this way. Tausk never had as close a personal relationship to Freud as did Adler, Jung, and Rank. Intense animosity developed between Freud and Tausk, but Tausk died too soon for it to flower into any major theoretical disputes.

Every man must, so Freud taught, in some sense slay his own father. A man of talent needs surrogate fathers, and Freud's genius certainly held forth an ideal of creativity for Tausk. If being mature means replacing one's father and his substitutes, a son must in some realm dare to surpass his models. Tausk struggled to grow away from Freud. He tried to divide Freud's psychological discoveries from Freud's personality, to tell himself that he had identified with psychoanalysis as a science but did not need Freud the man.

However, it was much harder in those days to make the distinction between Freud's writings and his personality. Devotion to psychoanalysis meant devotion to Freud, and vice versa. Whatever separation Tausk strove for between psychoanalysis and Freud himself could be only partially successful. For that whole generation Freud overshadowed psychoanalysis. And it was Freud, the first psychoanalyst, who was turning Tausk out, after he had accomplished so much for psychoanalysis.

However hard the line might have been to draw, one wonders how much Tausk ever had the will to draw it. Freud had in fact forced the issue. As with other men of ability, Tausk's troubles came partly from the discrepancy between his ambitions and his capacities. Now he had to find out whether he was capable of being creative without Freud. A man of forty had to try standing on his own two feet. Tausk might rationalize his refusal to lead a new school like Adler's or Jung's on the grounds that a public dispute with Freud, and the notoriety that went with it, would be too cheap a way out; one could win credit and fame simply by the publicity of the break itself. But these considerations can at best only partially explain what was also Tausk's own inability to be completely free.

Beneath all the bold and fiery elements in Tausk's life —his hatred of his father, his fight with his father-in-law, even his complaint against Martha that she had not been independent enough to be free—beneath all this clamorous striving for freedom lay deep passive cravings. Defiance as much as obedience can signify dependence. One of the tasks of growing up is confronting the problem of identifying with one's father, and when this is done it is no longer necessary to continue the struggle to be free of dependencies. Usually this happens in adolescence. While some may choose to seek out more gifted father surrogates in keeping with their own more exceptional capacities, eventually even the most talented man must stop searching for people to admire and emulate. Why after all does anyone hate his father? Because one loves him too much and does not get from him all that one wants.

Tausk obviously had tremendous yearnings for dependency, if not victimization. Though it was typical in families of that time for a son to defer to a father, Tausk's few surviving letters to Freud include almost childish accounts of how many patients he treated and what they suffered from. If Tausk had anyone to blame for such expectations of Freud, it should have been himself. But Tausk could lean so heavily on Freud all those years because he felt that at bottom Freud would hold him off. Freud's strength protected Tausk from the consequences of his passive tendencies, which interfered so cruelly in his relations with women.

For Tausk to have deserted Freud would have obviously been far healthier. Why could he not go elsewhere and practice, back to Berlin for instance? There was a good deal of moving about from Society to Society in those days, and usually it was the result of discontent with one psychoanalytic group or another. Why not simply go off to Yugoslavia as a psychiatrist? Although difficulties surrounded every alternative, the existence of these possibilities does illustrate the power of Tausk's dependent needs, which he had transferred onto Freud.

On the other hand, all of us live to some extent in closed worlds, and it is always easy for an outsider to spot the small pond in which someone else swims. From the point of view of an American, who has at least the illusion of such a variety of life choices, it is easy to underestimate

how simply one could be checkmated in Central Europe
fifty years ago. Psychiatry was the third career Tausk had
embarked on and the second for which he had undergone
rigorous training. Then, after having attacked the psychiatric status quo in Freud's behalf, he suddenly found
himself losing Freud—the great teacher under whose inspiration he had labored for the last ten years. It is not
difficult to understand how such a man might be at least
reluctant to begin anew, again.

Still, Tausk's great devotion and respect for Freud were
incongruous in a man of his age and talents. If Tausk
could not defect and leave Freud entirely, it was because
he had too many doubts of his own independent capacities. His relation to Freud had become symbiotic, and
Freud was an essential constituent of his work. Association
with Freud lifted all his followers to their creative best,
at the same time as it infantilized them vis-à-vis Freud
personally. It was no accident that legend has it that
Tausk castrated himself.

It may have been only when Freud finally brushed him
aside that Tausk was forced to realize how his tie to
Freud had masked his own inability to grow into independent manhood. But he had known all along that his
difficulty in establishing a secure relationship with a woman
was due to his inability to bear another person's dependency. Tausk's own dependencies were anxiety-ridden. Run-
ning from so many different women, Tausk was fleeing
from his own inner passivity.

Tausk was a man always in love. As Lou Andreas-
Salomé wrote of him, he was a "berserker with a tender

heart." With his whole succession of women, most of whom incidentally were Jewish,* each time he would get passionately involved for a fairly sustained period; and yet each time he drew back in fear. With women he could openly express his need for dependency, as well as the rebellion that it awoke in him. And so he deserted one woman after another, even though he was unable to take flight from Freud. Although Tausk was a "marrying man" who longed for the peace of family life, he could not maintain constant feelings toward someone he loved.

It is not clear how much Freud knew of Tausk's troubles with women. When Freud sent Tausk to Helene Deutsch for analysis, Freud spoke only about why he himself could not analyze him. Tausk's unstable and free attitude toward women, however, would not have endeared him to the puritanical and Victorian Freud.† His libido was so restlessly in search that it appears as if it were embarked on an inherently unsatisfiable quest for fulfillment. Tausk was a seeker, perhaps unconsciously of his sister Jelka. Yet the ideal he quested for must also have been an image within himself, which is why his search had to be so unending.

A contemporary of Tausk's, four years younger but also from Central Europe, shared his central conflicts. Though

---

* In addition to the women already mentioned, Tausk had been in love with Luci von Jacobi, Else Jerusalem, and Sonja Drublowicz.

† At Frankl-Hochwart's clinic Tausk once stimulated a woman's genitals with a galvanic rod after her ovaries had been removed, to see whether they retained their erotogenicity.

no Don Juan, Franz Kafka too was unable to go through with marriage; he too disappointed women in the same way. In addition, he could not detach himself from his father. Kafka looked on marriage as "the pledge of the most acute form of self-liberation and independence." But for him, as for Tausk, it was impossible to go through with it. "[F]rom the moment when I make up my mind to marry I can no longer sleep, my head burns day and night, life can no longer be called life, I stagger about in despair. . . . It is the general pressure of anxiety, of weakness, of self-contempt." "The fundamental idea of both [my] attempts at marriage was quite a right and proper one: to set up a house, to become independent."[18] But Kafka worried that his children might feel toward him as he had felt toward his father. Growing up would mean being the equal of his father, who still stood as the powerful giant of Kafka's childhood. So he failed to achieve the longed-for liberation.

One can wonder, with Kafka as with Tausk, whether their ties to their mothers, which they so rarely discuss, must also have played a role. For both men seemed to have a split in their love life; they could be fully potent as men only as long as there was no final commitment. Commitment to a woman can revive fears of a castrating mother image. Marriage can be the unconscious equivalent of castration since it means that now one cannot use one's penis freely: somebody has gained possession of it.

Although he did not share these obvious difficulties with marriage, Freud also—perhaps partly in the tradition of the nineteenth century—rarely discussed his tie to his mother, except in terms so unrealistically loving as to make one suspicious.* He never seems to have acknowledged how dependent on his mother he always was. She was in fact regal and self-sufficient, an opposite type from the woman he married, and the prototype of the kind of woman who in much later years would have power over him. Curiously enough for the discoverer of the Oedipus complex, Freud's mother was the dictatorial person, whereas his father seems to have been kindly and improvident.

In Freud's mind, however, like Kafka's and Tausk's, his father played an inordinately large role. Freud was forty years old when his father, an old man of eighty, died. Yet Freud wrote that this loss had "revolutionized my soul"[20] and made possible his discovery of the wish-fulfillment theory of dreaming.† Subsequently in Freud's theories mothers played a very small role, while he developed the importance of the child's tie to the father.

The precipitating cause of Tausk's suicide was certainly his inability to go through with his marriage to Hilde Loewi. We do not know much about the three-month

---

* "A mother is only brought unlimited satisfaction by her relation to a son; that is altogether the most perfect, the most free from ambivalence of all human relationships."[19]

† It may be that this loss can be connected to a falling off in Freud's sex life. Cf. Chap. ii, pp. 39–41. As Freud himself wrote of someone else, "he was the most pronounced rebel imaginable . . . on the other hand, at a deeper level he was still the most submissive of sons, who after his father's death denied himself all enjoyment of women out of a tender sense of guilt."[21]

period between the end of his analysis and his suicide. In that time he met this woman, once again fell in love, and made preparations to marry. But there is always a possibility of regression when falling in love. Freud had refused to analyze Tausk, and the analysis with Helene Deutsch was broken off before Tausk could be helped to overcome his recurrent problem with women.

We shall never know precisely what went on in Tausk's mind, and we cannot attempt more than an elucidation of some of the central threads that played their role. As Kafka put it, "Life is more than a Chinese puzzle."[22] Just before his intended marriage Tausk must have confronted the same anxiety and horror he had experienced at least twice before. He must have been faced with panic at what lay in store for him with Hilde. The notion of a lifetime with one woman was too much for him. On the one hand, he loved her too much to want to make her as unhappy as he had made Lea Rosen and Ilse Zimmerman, not to mention Martha. But on the other hand, he may have feared that he would be the one to become depressed, as after his affair in Lublin. In any event, life became more painful and tortured than death. Dying can be less threatening than living. So Tausk chose suicide.

CHAPTER V

Greatness of Achievement

1 *E*ven though fifty years have passed, we can fit together some of the pieces from Tausk's last day alive. The next morning he was to go for the marriage license. July 2, 1919, was a Wednesday. That day had special emotional meaning for psychoanalysts then, since Wednesday evenings were set aside for meetings of the Vienna Psychoanalytic Society.* But this particular week Tausk could not bear the prospect of attending Freud's group, and he sent a letter to Freud explaining his absence.

Vienna, July 2, 1919

Dear Professor,

Please excuse my absence from today's meeting. I am occupied in solving the decisive affairs of my life and I do not want by contact with you to be tempted to wish to resort to your help.

* The Boston Psychoanalytic Society still holds to the tradition of meeting Wednesday evening.

I shall probably soon be free again to approach you. I intend to appear with a minimum of neurosis.

In the meantime I remain with cordial respectful regards, gratefully yours

Tausk

Tausk knew he was in a crisis, but dared not go to the meeting for fear he would ask for Freud's help once more. He would not risk being rejected again. Over the years these Wednesday meetings had been the stage for Tausk's struggles with Freud.

The afternoon of July 2 Tausk spent with his seventeen-year-old son Marius, who had come from Graz for a visit and was preoccupied with his own young troubles. Although Marius had immense love and admiration for his father, he detected only that his father was rather worried. That night Tausk had supper with his son. Marius understood that his father was going to a concert later that evening, where Hilde Loewi was performing as an accompanist.

Tausk left his son with one bit of advice—that he not let his life be guided by too rigid principles. Tausk was ostensibly referring to Martha's antagonism toward alcohol. In a tactful way Tausk was trying to guide Marius away from his mother's rigidities without burdening his growing son. Doubtless with his own past problems in mind, Tausk encouraged Marius to be independent and not to imitate others too much. Perhaps Tausk's injunction was also a way of rationalizing his own failures as a father, by implying that at Marius's age he no longer needed parents. "Don't worry about me" were his last words to his son.

That evening Tausk wrote a letter to Nada, his favorite sister back in Yugoslavia, thanking her for sending him cigarettes (he smoked quite a lot) and bacon. He also told her of his forthcoming wedding. The letter was slightly pessimistic; she did not receive it until after his death. Apparently he had not yet decided to kill himself. His act was not premeditated, but in some sense had probably been preformed within him.

We do not know what happened later that night between Tausk and Hilde. Quite possibly she did nothing that might have realistically disturbed him. He must have realized, however, that although he had fallen in love with her partly to escape his dilemmas, he was nevertheless going to have them with him to the end. She was his hope, the last tie binding him to life. He had been using her to free himself from Freud, and presumably he realized that night that for him there was no way out. Despite his terrible longing for love, he found that he could not love Hilde.

His involvement with Freud had eaten up his emotional energy, and he had failed in his search for a solution to this conflict. As before, Tausk had fallen passionately in love, and then it had all disappeared. Late that Wednesday evening he was confronted with his commitment to marry. With this woman he had wanted more than ever to succeed in love, yet he knew that he had seen it all happening to him before. But this time he was left without Freud as well.

By the early morning hours of Thursday (July 3, 1919) Tausk had determined to kill himself. He wrote a will with a lengthy itemization of all his possessions, noting down even the smallest details. The huge inventory was all he had to establish his immortality.* In all that listing of his worldly goods, his decision stood. He also wrote and sealed two letters and left them on his desk—one to Hilde, the other to Freud. While completing this writing he sipped Slivovitz, the Yugoslav national drink. Then he tied a curtain cord around his neck, put his army pistol to his right temple, and pulled the trigger. Here was a man utterly determined to put an end to his life. Besides blowing off part of his head, as he fell he strangled himself.

Someone notified his sister Jelka, and her husband telegraphed to Graz that Victor was seriously ill. Although Marius had only just arrived back home, Martha set out immediately with her two boys. Ernst Gans ordered a second telegram to be sent within an hour, to tell them of Victor's death, but for some reason it was delayed. Not until she called at Jelka's in Vienna did Martha hear the news.

Within a couple of days Marius went to see Freud. If anyone could explain what had happened, the boy took

---

* Tausk's books, which filled nineteen boxes, were the most valuable part of his estate. His life insurance was consumed by the postwar inflation.

for granted that Freud would be the one. It was probably on the fifth of July that Marius was admitted to Freud's study for a short interview. Freud saw Marius between patients, and the boy understood what a privilege it was to be allowed into Freud's sanctuary. Freud was a bit standoffish, and the meeting was conducted on a formal and conventional plane. Of course Marius was only seventeen, and Freud would not have considered confiding in him. However, Freud did explain that he had received a suicide letter from Marius's father, and while Freud did not have it right at hand he would see to it that it was returned to Marius.

The funeral was set for July 6 at the Central Cemetery. There was no one to say a word about Tausk, neither priest nor rabbi—just the grave. Tausk's brother-in-law Hugo, Martha's brother, was particularly distraught—he wanted the coffin opened, he could not believe Victor was dead, since for him Victor had been the personification of life.

Families under stress are not always at their best. Martha managed to infuriate Ernst Gans by her deference to Hilde. Martha had wanted to share the first place at the burial with Hilde, but to Gans it seemed that this gesture to Victor's fiancée of a scant few months from the mother of Victor's sons showed insufficient respect for the dead man. Such a funeral for such a man was bound to leave them all shocked and with a sense of emptiness. In the few days before the funeral Hilde had tried to be cordial to Tausk's boys, but her own sense of numbness made all her efforts seem artificial.

Marius cannot quite remember now how it was that his father's letter to Freud was returned. He visited the Freud apartment again, and he thinks Anna Freud gave him back the precious note, along with some other correspondence of his father's. It might seem odd of Freud to give Marius his father's letters. What was the boy to do with them? Freud was not helping Marius in any way. But he was finishing getting rid of Victor Tausk. Yet Marius did not perceive any of this as inappropriate. Paradoxically, he treasured the suicide note for almost fifty years as a sign of his father's good relations with Freud.

Vienna, July 3, 1919

Dear Professor,

Please render assistance to my beloved fiancée, Miss Hilde Loewi (II Kornergasse 2), the dearest woman who ever entered into my life. She will not ask much of you, because she has a great capacity for happiness within herself, but she tends toward compulsive symptoms and identifications. She is noble, pure and kind, it is worth the trouble to give her good advice.

I thank you for all the good which you have done me. It was much and has given meaning to the last ten years of my life. Your work is genuine and great, I shall take leave of this life knowing that I was one of those who witnessed the triumph of one of the greatest ideas of mankind.

I have no melancholy, my suicide is the healthiest, most decent deed of my unsuccessful life. I have no accusations against anyone, my heart is without resentment, I am only dying somewhat earlier than I would have died naturally.

I greet the Psychoanalytic Association, I wish it well with all my heart. I thank all those who helped me when I was in need. Those who have claim to this gratitude will know it for themselves.

I hope you will have a long life, in health, strong and capable of working.

I greet you warmly.

Yours,

Tausk

Please, also look after my sons from time to time.

Having decided to kill himself, Tausk found inner reconciliation. With all his aggressive feelings directed inward, he was left with only love for others. The nearness of death appeased him, for he emphasizes how much he gained from Freud. There can be no mistaking what this letter amounts to. It is not addressed to the "most honored Professor" of his note to Freud earlier on Wednesday, but begins rather with "Lieber"—dear—Professor. The letter is a declaration of Tausk's love, yet without false intimacy, for it is signed "Tausk," since he was never "Victor" for Freud.

Tausk may have been about to kill himself like a wild animal, but what he left behind is serene and elevated. We have here the positive, aspiring side of his death—his thirst for immortality. With this letter he achieved his glory. However, the hurried signature is of a man who sees the image of himself fading.

Yet this suicide note had other overtones. In a sense it is really quite aggressive toward Freud. In the context

in which he wrote it, the letter also had the meaning—
"You think I want to kill you, when in fact I love and
admire you." By writing to Freud at all, Tausk is shifting
the blame for a lifetime's troubles. Wolfgang, Tausk's alter
ego in his play "Twilight," had said of himself, "whenever
I had a guilty conscience, then I wrote someone a beautiful
letter." Years before Tausk had had thoughts of suicide.
For almost eleven years he had managed to transmute
that haunting obsession into sacrifice for psychoanalysis.
The letter is so tranquil and normal. And yet he does not
say why. Tausk leaves Freud quite in the dark as to his
motivation for suicide.

For the last time Tausk uses a woman as a way to Freud.
In his letter Tausk is concerned only with the welfare of
others. He wants Freud to take care of other persons,
instead of himself. And so he recommends Hilde to Freud.
Perhaps Tausk had spoken well of her to Freud beforehand; but it is probably unlikely since Tausk had to give
her address so Freud could get in touch with her. Hilde
may never have seen Freud afterward. The channels between Tausk and Freud grew pathetically slight over the
years. First it had been Lou Andreas-Salomé, then Helene
Deutsch, and finally Hilde Loewi.

Tausk withheld his motivation from Freud, leaving it
enigmatic; but in the will he wrote early that last morning
of his life Tausk made clear at least his conscious motives.

I am taking leave of my life, which I have systematically
disintegrated ever since my childhood and which has now completely lost its sense since I can no longer enjoy it. My talent

is too little to support me. The recognition that I cannot gladly enter into a new marriage, that I can only keep myself and my beloved fiancée in conflicts and torments, is the true conscious motive of my suicide.

Good bye, mother, brothers, sisters and friends. Live better than I did, dear sons. Forget me all soon. I have deceived you all by living a role to which I was not equal.

One thinks back to his letter in 1905 in which he reported a friend's reproaches that he was mistaken in changing careers, that Victor Tausk was just a man like any other. Tausk had sacrificed so much to being a genius, and yet his capacities had not been great enough in his competition with Freud.

To obtain peace Tausk was bent on obliterating himself. He left instructions in his will for all his papers to be burned unread. (Kafka, incidentally, did likewise.) Hugo, Tausk's younger boy, spent a whole day fulfilling this request.

Tausk named Camillo Gans the executor of the will. As for his boys, Tausk appointed the psychoanalyst Edward Hitschmann their guardian. Hitschmann was a respected internist, introduced to psychoanalysis by his old friend Paul Federn. For a time he had been Freud's family doctor. Tausk asked Hitschmann to assist his sons "psychoanalytically since they are both more or less neurotic." Tausk had sought salvation in psychoanalysis, for himself and for those he loved. When his sister Nada had been in some difficulties, he recommended she go for treatment; and now he sent Hilde to Freud for advice. For Tausk psychoanalysis was not just a method of treatment for mental or spiritual problems, but the completion of education, the last solution to the problems of mankind.*

Apart from what Tausk wrote about the motives for his death, what can we infer from his whole life and his final predicament? Although many motives flow into the terrible inner loneliness preceding such an act, it should be possible to clarify some of the forces that released such immense cruelty. Tausk's anguish, and the part Freud played in it, by now are clear. Tausk's life had failed doubly, his home and his career. Unable to establish a lasting heterosexual relationship, Tausk's horror of ruining any more women's lives led him to reject his life ahead with Hilde. "No one gives up his life," it has been said, "who has not abandoned the hope for love."[2]

But Tausk had been in such a fury that he had killed himself in two ways, by shooting and hanging. It was a double suicide, which fit the two sides of his central conflict. In addition to his failure with Hilde, he was frustrated with Freud. If Tausk was killing himself rather than Hilde and Freud, then we can begin to understand this strange "double" death.†

---

* The reader should not assume that Tausk's outlook has disappeared even today. An analyst has recently (1965) maintained that "by the proper use of psychoanalysis, a new world, a new culture, and the means for the survival of the Occident could be built."[1]

† According to a colleague of Tausk's, Mela Pappenheim, the method of suicide which he chose had been described by their professor of forensic medicine as the surest way. So Tausk was in a sense simply doing what he had been taught.

A suicide, psychoanalysis has taught us, stems from aggression unable to turn outward. Wilhelm Stekel was the first to enunciate that "no one kills himself who did not want to kill another or, at least, wish death to another."[3] A suicide is a self-murder; murderer and murdered are combined in one person. One can identify with those one hates, as well as atone for the hateful wishes. As Freud put it in a paper just a few months after Tausk's death:

> . . . probably no one finds the mental energy required to kill himself unless, in the first place, in doing so he is at the same time killing an object with whom he has identified himself, and, in the second place, is turning against himself a death-wish which has been directed against someone else.[4]

Being dead, one cannot kill. And being dead, one cannot die. Suicide can be a means of mastering anxiety, of getting the better of existence.*

Tausk was no doubt afraid of his own will to live, and that is also why he had to make his act so decisive. People have been known to survive suicidal attempts after their gestures have gratified a passing self-destructive need. Most suicidal attempts have, in fact, a manipulative purpose; they aim to control other people in order to gratify certain wishes. In such cases the "consideration of death is, paradoxically, at a minimum."[5] Many suicidal people do not really want to die, or do not believe they will die as a consequence of their attempt. In fact, it turns out that rela-

---

* "What we call a suicide is for the individual himself an attempt to burst into life or to save his life. It may be to avoid something far more dreadful, to avoid committing murder or going mad."[6]

tively "few suicidal attempts are carried out in circumstances that would make death certain."[7] In Tausk's instance, however, the elements of attention-getting, play-acting, or even crying for help were less important than the pure unmitigated urge to die.

An objective link existed between the two people Tausk wanted dead, in that Freud had left him with his dilemma about women. Freud had refused to help him by an analysis. Tausk felt ready to become a beloved son of Freud's and then Freud put him off. It was no momentary suicidal impulse on Tausk's part. So much of his life had been bound up with being a psychoanalyst. Tausk lacked the strength of will, or the basic self-regard, to resist abdicating his humanity to Freud.

Tausk had been faced with starting all over again, finding a new profession for the third time. He could not leave, cease being a psychoanalyst, and still be productive. Yet he could not stay and fulfill his strivings for creation. By killing himself he could be reconciled with Freud as well as confirm his own guilt. On the one hand he could be rid of Freud's teachings only in that way; having identified with Freud so much, Tausk could slay him by suicide. On the other hand, by refusing the "easy" alternative of going off and founding his own school, Tausk could match his master's integrity.

Retrospectively it is all too easy to see the early signs that some people were not going to be able to make it successfully through life. Yet looking at the turning points in any lifetime, nothing ever seems as deterministic as it can be reconstructed after the fact. It is hard to say which is the more just, retrospection or contemporary judgment. It was true that Tausk had had serious conflicts throughout his life. He had had depressive moods and thoughts about death at least since the time he was writing lyric poetry. But he had won the love of many women, the admiration of colleagues, and the gratitude of patients. While a man of tremendous and primitive passions, it was only at the end that they decisively worked against him.

Freud set out to liberate, and yet Tausk had become enslaved. How then did Freud, at the age of sixty-three, react to the death of this outstanding pupil?

2 *F*reud's obituary presents one view. Though originally signed by an "editorial committee," it was subsequently included in a collection of Freud's works compiled under his own supervision, and so is now considered unquestionably by Freud himself.* The obituary excellently

---

* I am indebted here to a letter from James Strachey to me, January 28, 1967.

summarizes the changes in Tausk's career and his special addition to psychoanalytic thinking.

Among the sacrifices, fortunately few in number, claimed by the war from the ranks of psychoanalysis, we must count Dr. Victor Tausk. This rarely-gifted man, a Vienna specialist in nervous diseases, took his own life before peace was signed.

Dr. Tausk, who was only in his forty-second year, had for more than ten years been one of the closer circle of Freud's followers. Originally a lawyer by profession, he had for some considerable time been acting as a magistrate in Bosnia when, under the stress of severe personal troubles, he abandoned his career and turned to journalism, for which he was peculiarly suited by his wide general education. After working for some time as a journalist in Berlin, he came to Vienna in the same capacity. Here he became acquainted with psychoanalysis and soon decided to devote himself to it entirely. Although he was no longer a young man and was the father of a family, he was not deterred by the great difficulties and sacrifices involved in yet another change in profession, and one which must necessitate an interruption of several years before he could once more earn his living. For he embarked on the tedious study of medicine only as a means to enable him to carry on a psychoanalytic practice.

Shortly before the outbreak of the World War, Tausk had obtained his second doctor's degree and set up in Vienna as a nerve-specialist. Here, after a relatively short time, he had begun building up a considerable practice and had achieved some excellent results. These activities promised the rising young doctor full satisfaction as well as a means of support; but he was all at once violently torn from them by the war. He was called up immediately for active service and soon promoted to senior rank. He carried out his medical duties with devotion in the various theatres of war in the North and in the Balkans (finally in Belgrade), and received official commendation. It is also greatly to his honor that during the war he threw himself wholeheartedly, and with complete disregard of the consequences, into exposing the numerous abuses which so many doctors unfortunately tolerated in silence or for which they even shared the responsibility.

The stresses of many years' service in the field could not fail to exercise a severely damaging psychological effect on so intensely conscientious a man. At the last Psychoanalytical Congress, which we held in Budapest in September 1918 and which brought analysts together once more after many years of separation, Dr. Tausk, who had long been suffering from physical ill-heath, was already showing signs of unusual nervous irritability. When, soon afterwards, in the late autumn of last year, he came to the end of his military service and returned to Vienna, he was faced for the third time, in his state of mental exhaustion, with the hard task of building up a new existence —this time under the most unfavorable internal and external conditions. In addition to this, Dr. Tausk, who has left two grown-up sons to whom he was a devoted father, was on the brink of contracting a new marriage. He was no longer able to cope with the many demands imposed on him in his ailing state by harsh reality. On the morning of July 3rd he put an end to his life.

Dr. Tausk had been a member of the Vienna Psychoanalytical Society since the autumn of 1909. He was well known to the readers of this journal from his numerous contributions, which were distinguished by sharp observation, sound judgment and a particular clearness of expression. These writings exhibit plainly the philosophical training which the author was able so happily to combine with the exact methods of science. His strong need to establish things on a philosophical foundation and to achieve epistemological clarity compelled him to formulate, and seek as well to master, the whole profundity and comprehensive meaning of the very difficult problems involved. Perhaps he sometimes went too far in this direction, in his impetuous urge for investigation. Perhaps the time was not yet ripe for laying such general foundations as these for the young science of psychoanalysis. The psychoanalytic consideration of philosophical problems, for which Tausk showed special aptitude, promises to become more and more fruitful. One of his last works, on the psychoanalysis of the function of judgment, which was delivered at the Budapest Congress and has not yet been published, gives evidence of this direction taken by his interest.

In addition to his gift for philosophy and attraction towards it, Tausk possessed a quite exceptional medico-psychological capacity and produced some excellent work in that field too. His clinical activities, to which we owe valuable researches into various psychoses (e.g., melancholia and schizophrenia), justified the fairest hopes and gave him the prospective appointment to a University Lectureship for which he had applied.

All those who knew him well value his straightforward character, his honesty towards himself and towards others and the superiority of a nature which was distinguished by a striving for nobility and perfection. His passionate temperament found expression in sharp, and sometimes too sharp, criticisms, which however were combined with a brilliant gift for exposition. These personal qualities exercised a great attraction on many people, and some, too, may have been repelled by them. No one, however, could escape the impression that here was a man of importance.

How much psychoanalysis meant for him, even up to his last moments, is shown by letters which he left behind, in which he expressed his unreserved belief in it and his hope that it will find recognition at a not too distant date. There is no doubt that this man, of whom our science and his friends in Vienna have been prematurely robbed, has contributed to that aim. He is sure of an honorable memory in the history of psychoanalysis and its earliest struggles.[8]

External circumstances, according to Freud, claimed Tausk's life. Although Freud delineates the stresses under which Tausk lived, Freud does not really interweave Tausk's inner feelings with the calamity of the world war. Yet as Freud well knew, when one is deeply troubled reality problems can be surprisingly comforting. In blaming Tausk's death on the war, Freud was not consciously dissembling. He really wanted to think that he played no part in Tausk's final tragedy. Freud may have been shocked at Tausk's unexpected death, even if he did not allow himself to grieve.

We do not know, since the particular passages have not been published, what Freud wrote to his pupils Abraham and Ferenczi about the incident. But there is a bit in a letter to Pfister on July 13, ten days after Tausk's death, which is fully consistent with the themes of his obituary. "Dr. Tausk has committed suicide. He was a highly gifted man, but was a victim of fate, a delayed victim of the war. Did you know him?"[9]

On July 15, 1919, Freud left for the beginning of his summer vacation with his sister-in-law, Minna. His wife stayed home, as Minna was always more of an intellectual companion, and he regularly traveled with her. Freud waited almost a month after Tausk's death until he wrote to Lou Andreas-Salomé, on August 1. Freud will be remembered as one of the world's great letter writers. When he was at work, he regularly set aside time in which he freely wrote a stack of letters. Through his letter writing he kept in touch with followers all over the world. (Jung, for example, often annoyed Freud because he was less dedicated to the art of letter writing.)

In his note to Lou about Tausk, Freud again deceived himself by denying any responsibility for Tausk's death. Had he known what he had helped to do to Tausk, Freud would never have written that obituary or returned that suicide letter to Tausk's son. To Lou Freud could be far more open concerning his relief that Tausk was finally gone.

Poor Tausk, whom you distinguished a while with your friendship, put a thorough end to his life on July 3. He came back from the horrors of war exhausted, set out under the most unfavorable circumstances to reconstruct the existence he had lost through his military duty, made an attempt to take a new woman into his life, was due to marry one week later—but decided otherwise. His farewell letters to his fiancée, to his first wife, and to me are all alike affectionate, attest his lucidity, blame no one but his own inadequacy and bungled life—thus throw no light on the final deed. In the letter to me he avers steadfast fidelity to psychoanalysis, thanks me, etc. But how it might have looked behind that is not to be guessed. So he fought out his day of life with the father ghost. I confess I do not really miss him; I had long taken him to be useless, indeed a threat to the future. I had a chance to cast a few glances into the substructure on which his proud sublimations rested; and would long since have dropped him had *you* not so boosted him in my esteem. Of course I was ready anyhow to do what I could for him, only I have been quite powerless of late given the degeneration of all relations in Vienna. I never failed to recognize his significant gift, but it was prevented from being translated into correspondingly valuable achievements.

Freud's letter would be shocking even if we had not followed Tausk's tragedy so closely. Unfortunately, as with all the censorship of Freud's letters, the most offending passages have been excised from the version of this letter already published.[10] Admittedly any letter is a special means of communication, as much for oneself as for the recipient. There may well have been unspoken assumptions about Tausk between Freud and Lou. And Freud was characteristically honest about his feelings, courageous about some of his worst qualities—which is exactly what has laid him so open to criticism. He prided himself on his integrity, on the complete identity between what he said and believed.

But no matter how one leans over backwards to Freud regarding his relation to Tausk, this letter to Lou seems inhuman. Contrasting it with Tausk's own last letter to Freud, it is scarcely credible that Freud could have uttered such thoughts. In contrast to Freud's obituary, with all its public praise, in private Freud was left with only pity for Tausk. Freud, who lived for self-knowledge, seemed to care more for what was "useful" to his studies than for a human life. His dedication to the cause of psychoanalysis sanctioned this ruthlessness.*

As a young man, before founding psychoanalysis, Freud would not have been so heartless in the face of human tragedy; at the age of twenty-seven he wrote a remarkably sensitive and feeling letter to Martha about a friend's suicide.[11] Freud possessed all the psychological talents of a great writer. But as he aged, and the more the scientist in him triumphed over the artist, his humanity grew restricted. Psychoanalysis, he later wrote, had "become my whole life to me."[12]

Freud was quite right to doubt the surface of Tausk's suicide note; well might he suspect that more lay behind it. As far as possible, though, Freud completely spares himself blame, while writing to Lou for confirmation. As far as we know, Freud was wrong in thinking there was another letter to Martha. Freud may have wanted to diffuse the responsibility for the suicide among as many people around Tausk as possible (just as initially Freud's obituary was signed by an "editorial committee" instead

---

* Might it have been of Tausk's suicide that Hanns Sachs wrote: "I saw him [Freud] when the news came that someone with whom he had been on friendly terms for years had committed suicide. I found him strangely unmoved by such a tragic event." Sachs: *Freud, Master and Friend*, p. 147.

of himself). It is unlikely that Freud saw the letter to Hilde or the supposed one to Martha, otherwise why would they not have told Freud of the conscious motive Tausk had declared in his will? Or was Freud unwilling to accept that version of Tausk's act?

Freud's obituary had praised Tausk for all his many gifts and contributions. By stressing Tausk's "philosophical" mind Freud was paying him a backhanded compliment, for Freud strove to emancipate psychology from its metaphysical associates and to found psychoanalysis on an empirical basis. He is reported to have said many times that he "heartily abhorred philosophy." Although he himself could soar to abstract heights, the category of "a speculation" could always be used to damn a new idea.*

Freud was writing to Lou in puzzlement; Tausk's death seemed enigmatic. When Freud declared Tausk was a "threat to the future," what could he have meant? Tausk was not yet in the line of succession, as Adler or Jung had been. Brilliant though Tausk was, he would have to have played a much greater role in psychoanalysis than he did to justify any fears that he might distort psychoanalysis after Freud's death. Tausk was more a nuisance and personal threat to Freud than a real competitor in the world of psychoanalysis.

But if Freud considered Tausk "useless," it was surely only for Freud's own glory and not for science. Had he lived, Tausk could still have contributed much. Yet psychoanalysis was Freud's own creation, and it was tempting

---

* For Freud's ambivalence toward philosophy and social theory, cf. my *Freud: Political and Social Thought,* pp. 101-10.

for him to believe that what was "useless" to him personally was objectively without value. Anyone who has ever put his own ego into work may perhaps share something of Freud's sensitivity to criticism.

There really was something uncanny in the relationship between Freud and Tausk. For as if in continuation of their tie, at the time Tausk killed himself Freud was beginning to formulate the concept of a death instinct. In the very same letter to Lou telling of Tausk's suicide, Freud alludes to stumbling across a new aspect of the "death theme," "an amazing idea hailing from the instincts." Freud had been intrigued by the psychology of death for some time, as had a whole tradition within German literature. But his explicit postulation of an instinct of primitive destructiveness came simultaneously with Tausk's suicide. One can only wonder whether Tausk had heard—or intuited—anything about it from Freud. Could Tausk have been acting out Freud's newest, or even just barely burgeoning, idea? Or perhaps the notion of a death instinct represented another way for Freud to deny any responsibility for Tausk's suicide.[13]

3   *L*ou was taken aback by Freud's cold portrayal of Tausk's death. Yet her reply by letter was a masterpiece of subtle diplomacy with Freud. At the same time her letter expresses her continued appreciation of Tausk's character.

She delayed her reply until August 25, the anniversary of Nietzsche's death.

Your notification took me altogether by surprise. Poor Tausk. I was fond of him. Believed I knew him; yet would never, never have thought of suicide (successful suicide—not attempts or threats I mean—strikes me almost rather as a proof of health than the contrary). Actually I cannot even guess which means he chose (poison would have been ever so easy for him, a doctor, to obtain); if he chose a weapon, then I could imagine that this death was the ultimate in voluptuous gratification for him as aggressor *and* sufferer in one. For here lay the Tausk problem, his danger, which at the same time constituted his charm (unpsychoanalytically, he might be called a berserker with a tender heart). What you write—that basically you do not miss him—seems to me not merely understandable; I too felt him to be a certain "threat to the future" to you as also to the cause that consciously he championed with such enthusiasm and sincerity. He knew of my misgivings about him, my dread lest he insist on a university appointment in Vienna. In March he wanted to come to [me in] Munich, but I was against it; I did not answer his last letter, like so many before it, and he was right when he wrote a year ago, "No one will sit down at the same table with a wretch: not even you have done so." No, not even I.

The true sufferer as also the true beloved in this case is Jelka, his sister. I would like to write to her, I think, if I knew her Vienna address and her husband's name; but it has slipped my memory.[14]

Lou by and large falls in with Freud's interpretation of Tausk's character, yet she manages to shift slightly the center of gravity of the post-mortem to Tausk's lovableness.

She maintains, in parentheses to be sure, that "unpsycho-analytically" Tausk was a "berserker with a tender heart" —what she means is that you, Freud, and psychoanalysis, your science, might have some labels for him, but humanly his best qualities made him vulnerable to victimization. The world of grown-ups can cripple our most human qualities. Lou concentrates not just on Tausk's struggle with the "father ghost," but on his tender affection for Jelka. Tausk was a man who could trust his character less than his intellect. As Lou remarks of Tausk in a marginal comment on her letter, "even such a *strong* character dwarfs to powerlessness when confronting the inner giants of immoderation."

Evidently in March 1919, when his analysis was broken off, Tausk turned to Lou for sustenance. Although at least Lou acknowledges feeling badly about abandoning Tausk to his fate, and although she softens the force of Freud's dismissal of Tausk as a human being, she picks up Freud's theme that Tausk was a menace to the future of psycho-analysis. She accepts Freud's flattery that it was because of her befriending Tausk that Freud put up with him for so long. She had fondness for Tausk, not love. In fact, she gives him up so readily, defending him so little, that one can only conclude that she may have really used Tausk all along for the sake of her relationship to Freud. She had taken Tausk as a lover as second best. According to her latest biographer, up to her death in 1937 Lou (who had become a practicing psychoanalyst) never wrote another word about Tausk to Freud.

Freud had not been explicit with Lou about how Tausk had chosen to die. And with Helene Deutsch he did not choose to discuss what had happened. She was away in the country when Tausk died. Afterwards she said to Freud that perhaps if she had kept Tausk in analysis, if she had not sent him away, he would still be alive. Freud dodged her remorseful query by saying coldly—"But you made the right choice, you chose for yourself." He gave her, in other words, permission not to be guilty, not to grieve. On the other hand, perhaps he was trying to protect her from feeling too guilty.

For Helene Deutsch certainly had played a greater part in Tausk's undoing than she was then aware. Of course she could not have known for what purposes Freud might be using her vis-à-vis Tausk. She was new and inexperienced as an analyst. The deep impression Tausk's suicide made on her is in fact not unlike the scar many psychiatrists bear from a suicide early in their training. But in Helene's case, because she was in analysis with Freud and therefore so deferential to him, it seemed to her as if the suicide were not her responsibility but Freud's. Just as Freud put the blame for Tausk's death elsewhere, on the war, Helene put whatever blame there was on Freud.

Of course in retrospect it was not unreasonable for her to have considered her own role negligible, a mere mediator between Tausk and Freud.* On the surface, little

---

* Ruth Mack Brunswick, when she had Freud's former patient, the "Wolf-man," in analysis in the 1920's, wrote that she had been a mere channel between the patient and Freud.[15]

emotional tie between patient and analyst, the famed "transference," ever got established between Tausk and Helene.

However, in a subtle way Tausk had been wooing his analyst with the story of his conflict with the master. The tale of his difficulties with Freud was the most seductive power Tausk had at his disposal. Tausk's resentment of Freud was such an exciting contrast to Helene's own adoration of "Professor"; she could indulge her interest in this rebellious pupil without ever acknowledging to herself that she too might have any such critical feelings about Freud. All her own negative impulses to Freud could be isolated and embodied in the person of Tausk. Going to Freud with Tausk's story, Helene was unintentionally betraying her patient; she was showing herself as the good pupil, not like the assertive and troublesome Tausk. For all we know, she may have implicitly encouraged Tausk's interest in her own analyst, and his expressions of rivalry.

It is impossible to overestimate the role of human vanity in life. Tausk may have known Helene well as a person, but as he lay on her couch, talking about his predicament, his own egoism made her into a figure of great emotional importance to him. Each of us nurses a tremendous amount of self-importance, most of it usually latent and under control. Psychoanalysis as a therapy aims to activate these unconscious feelings, and then help give the patient distance toward them. But in this process the lowliest analyst becomes a god to his patient.

As a method of treatment psychoanalysis aims to be the least manipulative of therapies; the patient, through rational understanding, becomes his own best self. Yet the analytic situation all too often contains hidden elements of suggestion, which can elude both patient and analyst. The general silence, for example, ensures a disproportionate weight to each of the analyst's comments. Just as Freud took Helene's immense admiration as fully justified in reality, needing no dissolution through interpretations, so Helene never realized how Tausk was flattering her by his tale, or how she might be benefiting by it all in Freud's eyes.[16]

Freud's whole system of thought gave him (and later therapists) too many intellectual options, and too few restraints, whenever his own ego (and that of all later therapists) asserted itself. Any psychotherapist can only be checked by his own sense of responsibility. As Freud sadly wrote many years later, in his extreme old age, when he was altogether more pessimistic about the therapeutic results of analysis, "when a man is endowed with power it is hard for him not to misuse it."[17]

From Freud's point of view, he had not simply thrown Tausk away, but had sent him to someone in whom he had confidence. It would be a way, he might tell himself, of watching over the case. It was so easy to rationalize keeping Tausk at a distance. Patients should be neurotic, not analysts. Little of what Freud did to Tausk was deliberate sadism; there was no special pleasure in his cruelty to Tausk.

But the cruelty was so built into the situation that none

of the participants had to realize what had happened. The last thing one should do to a suicidal or depressive patient is to send him away. Since neither Freud nor Helene ever recognized that Tausk was so badly off, the message for him to go kill himself may not have been so clear.

But the analysis itself had done harm. Freud would have been the first to maintain that unless analysis can hurt, it does not have the power ever to help. "[I]f a knife does not cut, it can not be used for healing either."[18] Psychoanalysis is designed to induce a regression in a patient; it has been compared to a slow-motion hypnosis. The treatment is supposed to activate conflicts, for a constructive purpose. Whatever suggestibility is built into the process is supposed to be contained within the therapeutic alliance between analyst and patient.

Classical analysis, however, with the couch and the neutral analyst, may arouse so much regression and dependency in the patient, hidden as well as open, that the patient becomes unable to cope with it, and the analyst is not equipped to meet it either. The structure of the analytic situation can always deceive one into thinking that it is less close and intimate than the formal arrangements make it appear. It is the impersonality of the analyst, out of sight and aloof, which makes it possible for some patients to open up in the first place. A patient is especially vulnerable in the early stages of an analysis, and just at that point Tausk was abruptly dismissed.

These three brilliant people were playing with human dynamite. Having permitted them all to be so close, Freud suddenly tried to be distant. It would be no wonder if Tausk's murderous rage were aroused. We may speculate that from Tausk's point of view it was as if father had rejected him for interfering with mother's relationship to father. And in the end father took mother away, keeping her for himself.

Of course any analysis, just as it can accomplish a limited amount of good, can only do a finite amount of harm. But Tausk was entitled to his fury, especially against himself. Instead of coming back from the war and struggling on his own to put his life back together again, he had turned to Freud, whose coolness toward him must have been apparent, for help. And well might he rage against both female and male images from the past, and their proto-types in the present, Helene and Freud. They had con-tributed to his end, first by helping to mobilize all his transference expectations, for any analysis, after all, is sup-posed to stir up magical feelings in a patient. But then they interrupted his analysis without finding any other compro-mise. Freud used to quote a saying of Lessing's: "A person who does not lose his reason under certain conditions can have no reason to lose."

4 *E*veryone in the inner circle of psychoanalysts shared a sense of shock at Tausk's suicide. One might expect only the court flatterers to have sided with Freud. But, as we have seen, to be an analyst at all then meant living in a small minority, on the defensive and under attack. It was natural to adopt Freud's truculence toward the outside world. The ties binding psychoanalysts together were as strong as their hostility to the nonanalytic world. It becomes easy to hate anyone who diverges even slightly from so cohesive a group, and anything that smacks of compromise with the enemy can seem a betrayal of the cause.

Unfortunately we have only one letter from a member of Freud's circle that gives an account of what happened, but it goes far to confirm the narrative already reconstructed. Paul Federn sent it to his wife Wilma on the very day Tausk's body was discovered. She was off in the country, but he felt he had to write to her right away, even though he would be seeing her that Saturday.

Federn was an internist who had come to Freud's group in 1903, one of the earliest of Freud's followers. He was also one of Tausk's closest friends. They had had their difficulties, especially over Tausk's flirtation with Wilma, who was much younger than her husband. But Federn deeply admired Tausk's work, especially as he too was interested in applying the insights of psychoanalysis to the treatment of psychotics. Federn's version counts not only because he was so close to the scene, but also because he himself possessed a richness of psychological talent.

Federn was a born idealist and politically an active man of the Left. His mission was to cure, and he was convinced that psychoanalysis was the final message of liberation for mankind. "One could wish that many poets, founders of religions, and other men of stature had submitted to therapy; then they might have accomplished great things."[19] Federn traveled from Vienna to New York City before World War I to treat the stammer of a wealthy young American, who later became governor of New York and a United States senator—Herbert H. Lehman.

"Federn was a romanticist and reformer, Freud a realist and searcher."[20] As Freud thought there was little possibility of improving mankind, understandably enough tensions existed between the two men. Federn often mentioned, with great sadness, his regret and resentment that Freud had not taken him into analysis.* Like Tausk, Federn yearned for more from Freud, at the same time as he felt his independence cramped in Freud's circle.

But to the end Federn was Freud's devoted apostle. To the generation of analysts who came in the 1920's and 1930's, Federn was a patriarch, the St. Peter of the movement. Federn felt himself a traitor to his own father, so there was something sacred in his relation to Freud. There are many stories about Federn's piety toward Freud. According to one, years after Freud's death Federn approached a portrait of Freud murmuring "master, master." And according to another, Federn's wife had a maxim for her children—"First comes God, then Freud, and then your father." An offense to his friend Tausk would have to be very gross before he would permit a critical comment about Freud to enter his head.

---

* In the case of Wilhelm Reich, one of the most promising psychoanalysts of a later generation, "it was the refusal of Freud to take Reich for personal analysis that led to the serious break. . . . The rejection, as Reich felt it, was intolerable. Reich reacted to this rejection with deep depression." Ilse Ollendorff Reich: *Wilhelm Reich* (New York: St. Martin's Press; 1969), p. 14.

Our cares weigh heavily because things are now such that often one really cannot carry on.—I have much to tell you. Most of it I leave for my verbal report on Saturday.

I must write you the worst. Today Tausk shot himself. I don't yet know anything more detailed. Hitschmann happened to call him, the ambulance was just there. He was not at the meeting yesterday. I am certain that being destitute and unable to borrow money for enough to eat was but the last push. The motivation was Freud's turning away from him. It is a thousand pities for this superior, talented, and high meaning man. I am so terribly sorry about him. If I had been able, I would certainly have helped him, although he always bit the hand that reached out to help him. I had forgiven him inwardly, but I was no longer fond of him after the time he so insulted me, and at every opportunity—even after Budapest—whenever I approached him in a friendly way I found only vanity, envy, and lack of interest. If Freud had shown him a human interest, not simply recognition and support, he might have continued to bear longer his martyr-like existence. Because for a man of his sensitivity of mind, this kind of looking for bread was martyrdom just as it is for you. But *he* was not *kind* as little as Freud is kind, i.e. Freud possesses so much love for people that he can be kind, but in his old age he became increasingly harder—and this is understandable with Freud because he, too, had to live a life unworthy of his greatness.—That we could not keep Tausk is our shame. However, he made enemies for himself everywhere and always; at the end he drove his psychological patients away, apparently in order to demonstrate the uselessness of the method, out of rancour against Freud. The methodological rigor which Freud teaches makes people hard and alienates them from their fellow men; he who cannot love is defenseless against failure.—Dr. Josef Frey is the same kind of person but borne up by an interest in the common welfare. To this Tausk could not ascend. And yet what a pity for this great mind and artistic powers.

On July 8 Federn again referred to Tausk in a letter to his wife: "I am maddeningly busy, partially, but to a smaller part, because I treat a patient of Tausk's. I think of him often and don't dare to visit his people. Also because I cannot be frank with them about everything."

Unlike Lou, Federn was objective enough, and sufficiently Tausk's friend, to be able to do more—at least in writing to his wife—than just take Freud's side, although he acknowledged how impossible Tausk could be at times. Yet Freud was so much God to Federn that he could not be frank with Tausk's family. It is questionable, though, how realistic Tausk's misery could have been. Food was scarce, but he had friends who could help him; Jelka lived in Vienna, and she could keep him alive—although she disapproved of the match with Hilde. Tausk's unhappiness was not simply a reaction to the stress of external conditions. His problem was more his inner despair.

But Tausk was a proud man, and seeking support at his age meant humiliation for him. The greatest enemy of mankind may not be aggression, but what Christians have all along considered "pride" and what psychoanalysts have chosen to rename "narcissism." Each humiliation only aggravated Tausk's vanity. His self-love was the equivalent of his self-contempt.

Federn knew what he was talking about when he said that Tausk always bit the hand that fed him. Tausk said as much about himself when he came to understand his difficulties with Martha in terms of his own problems in tolerating dependency. He could treat with the greatest arrogance those who were trying hardest to help him. But Tausk's brutality toward Federn may have been spurred on in part by Freud's own obvious discontent with his early Viennese followers.

Tausk was assuredly no easy man to get along with. As students of Freud Tausk and Federn were rivals. A letter of Tausk's on May 3 indicated that his summer vacation was in doubt because his practice was shaky, so he may well have been driving away patients out of anger against Freud. Unlike Tausk, Federn was able to be the devoted apostle; he knew some of his limitations and was able to make the most of the gifts that he had. Tausk, however, wanted more.

At the risk of making this whole group seem even wilder than they were, it should be added here that years later Federn too shot himself. He was then a very old man, seventy-nine, and his wife had already died. He was also suffering from cancer of the bladder. A short time before he had endured an operation for this cancer, which failed in its purpose but had precipitated a temporary psychosis. Such a mental disorder following a serious operation is far more common than is popularly known; it can be an organic process, or even represent a fight for life. When his wound healed, Federn recovered fully. But he was then scheduled for another such operation; he killed himself the morning he was to be sent to the hospital.

Federn could not face another postoperative breakdown. He wanted to avoid mental and physical crippledom. It is a medical fiction, based on the doctor's commitment to save life, that suicide is inherently irrational or unhealthy. Federn arranged for all his patients to be transferred to other therapists, and then shot himself sitting in his analytic chair in the early morning hours of May 4, 1950. Like his friend Tausk, Federn died after a Wednesday evening. In the suicide note Federn left for his sons, he recurred to his romantic image of himself as a soldier, "the long-serving sergeant in the psychoanalytic army." Again like Tausk, Federn had never become a deserter.

How could Freud have ever gotten so much power over these people? Tausk not only permitted himself to be crushed, but Federn flatly asserts that the motive for the suicide was Freud's rejection. Tausk's quarrel with Freud need never have been kept such a secret, except for the need to make Freud so potent. Any organization has its "secrets," usually pretty banal ones; *why* something is considered a secret, however, is another matter. Federn, as well as others in that tiny subculture, readily believed that if Freud dropped a man it could lead to his self-extinction. Exclusion from the revolutionary community was an annihilation greater than any physical death.

Realistically, Freud was the analyst each of them turned to in their difficulties. He helped Federn, for example, when his marriage grew troubled. But the awe these people had for Freud surpassed anything he did for them in reality. They awaited each of his papers as they appeared with the same anticipation due the birth of a child. They made his every wish into a command. King Henry is supposed to have breathed with a sigh that Becket be dispatched; so if Freud wanted Tausk dead, it seemed perfectly in order for Tausk to oblige. Freud had such tremendous power over them because they all wanted to have it so.

Freud ejected at least one other pupil who reacted very much like Tausk. Herbert Silberer, another early supporter of Freud's, became depressed in the early 1920's over his relationship with Freud. Silberer felt very offended and rejected by Freud's attitude toward him. No one knew then why Freud did not like Silberer; he was devoted to Freud and had done important work, but Freud was not friendly or receptive to him.[21] Freud's rejection was quite open, although just how curt Freud's dismissal could be was not.

In a letter to Silberer (which Freud's official biographer, Ernest Jones, chose not to make use of) Freud wrote:

April 17, 1922

Dear Sir,

I request that you do not make the intended visit with me. As the result of the observation and impressions of recent years I no longer desire personal contact with you.

Very truly yours,

Freud

Silberer killed himself nine months later.

Although not much more is known of Silberer's problems, certainly Tausk circled toward Freud like a moth around a flame. Tausk's neurosis involved his whole personality; every piece of him was consumed in the struggle with Freud. His destruction at Freud's hands seemed irresistible. Tausk's gypsy tale of 1906, "Husein Brko," had raised the theme of a father slaying his son.

But an even more striking literary parallel appears in a story by Kafka, whose suffering was so similar to Tausk's. In his short story "The Judgment," an angry father "sentences" his son to death by drowning; the son immediately complies by rushing from his father's house to a bridge from which he jumps to his death in the waters below.

Freud was irresistibly seductive to this whole group of people, and part of his power came from the ease with which he was able to wield it. Freud disliked infatuations, yet he aroused them, especially in those with the fewest defenses. In encouraging Tausk to join the psychoanalytic movement, Freud had been quite active and solicitous. He had done everything for Tausk as a psychoanalyst—subsidized his medical education, made him editor of a journal, sent him patients. But Freud did this more for the cause than for the man, and when Tausk began to infuriate him, he simply brushed Tausk aside. Freud reigned effortlessly. Tausk may have acted like a moth, but Freud was a flame.

Freud had his mission; his work was the center of his

life, and he saw everything else around it much less clearly. In part Freud preferred to be unaware of his power over his followers. Power can infantilize those who wield it as much as those who submit to it. If some of his followers got crushed, well, that was too bad. But he could not allow them to become a burden to him. Had Freud chosen, he might well have been able to save Tausk, but taking him into analysis would have been a challenge and a sacrifice.

Devotion to a cause not only sanctioned disregard for human life, but also permitted Freud genuine humility. To the end of his life Freud thought his discovery of psychoanalysis had been a piece of good luck: he was a simple man with a great subject. It was not false modesty that moved Freud to reject the notion that he was a great man.

I have a high opinion of what I have discovered, but not of myself. Great discoverers are not necessarily great men. Who changed the world more than Columbus? What was he? An adventurer. He had character, it is true, but he was not a great man. So you see that one may find great things without its meaning that one is really great.[22]

Perhaps it was some inner glimmering of his own human failings out of which his triumph had been forged that led Freud on another occasion to observe:

It has always seemed to me that ruthlessness and arrogant self-confidence constitute the indispensable condition for what, when it succeeds, strikes us as greatness; and I also believe that one ought to differentiate between greatness of achievement and greatness of personality.[23]

As Lou Andreas-Salomé remarked of Freud, "confronted by a human being who impresses us as great, should we not be moved rather than chilled by the knowledge that he might have attained his greatness only through his frailties?"[24]

CHAPTER VI

Free Associations

*W*hile each of us is likely to interpret Tausk's life on the basis of quite personal lessons derived from our own experience, the historian should aim to use the Tausk story as a key to understanding Freud's life and career. With this purpose in mind, we shall examine first how the pattern of Freud's anxiety over Tausk's possible plagiarism recurs whenever Freud had difficulties with his students. Next, Freud's fascination with thought-transference will lead us to an interpretation of how he came to discover the technique of free associations. And finally, Tausk's own special contribution to psychotherapy will be contrasted with Freud's practice as an analyst.

*1   I*n 1911 Freud had his famous controversy with Alfred Adler, who until then had been one of his closest disciples. Just as Freud could interpret intellectual differences as personal affronts, here personal issues mushroomed into a theoretical debate. And in this instance Freud decided it was better to force the issue, and split his Society, than to let Adler's views get mixed up with his own.

Everyone in the Society had to take a stand, one way or the other. Tausk at this date fought loyally by Freud's side. Freud violently denounced Adler; it was a trial, and the accusation was heresy.* As Freud examined Adler's views, he picked over those concepts that Adler claimed to have fostered. What seemed new, Freud claimed, was trivial, and the rest had been taken from Freud without acknowledgment.[1]

The penalty was excommunication, and Freud ostracized Adler and his sympathizers. By the end of these meetings, having driven out even some neutrals in the dispute, Freud was boiling at what he considered Adler's betrayal. There were always at least two Freuds, one cool and rational, the other terribly furious and afraid. As with each of his deviating pupils, Freud had a psychopathological label at hand: Adler was, Freud wrote, a malicious paranoiac.[2]

---

* Although Richard Wagner voted with Freud, and Paul Klemperer with Adler, both agreed the meetings were a "trial." They differed, however, in how personal Freud had made his attack on Adler.[3]

Curiously enough, Freud, who had advised his students not to squander their creative energies, at the same time criticized Adler for being too single-minded. This charge of reductionism has been reiterated against all the "deviationists" in psychoanalysis down to our own day. The theme of plagiarism echoes in all this. The unity was Freud's, and Adler had taken a part of it. Not only had Adler thrown "all the psychological discoveries of psychoanalysis to the winds," but "what he had rejected forced its way back into his closed system under other names. . . ."[4] In later years Freud frequently maintained that his students were "like dogs. They take a bone from the table, and chew it independently in a corner. But it is my bone!"

People do have difficulty being grateful to benefactors, as Freud knew from his own hatred of depending on his teachers; it would be only human for Adler to share this fault, and for Freud in turn to be resentful. Adler tried to justify his discontent by saying to Freud, "Do you think it gives me such great pleasure to stand in your shadow my whole life long?"[5] Tausk later shared this same discomfort.

Just as Freud jockeyed with predecessors over priorities, so he disliked what he called Adler's "uncontrolled craving for priority."[6] Adler, like Tausk later on, made claims to discoveries of his own which Freud refused to acknowledge. Of this controversy Adler once wrote to Lou, "My opinions might be wrong! But is that a good enough reason to steal them too?"[7]

Every subculture has its villains, and among Freud's descendents Adler's role is a closed story of a disciple's ingratitude. Freud is supposed to have been a bad judge of character, betrayed by those he helped most. For those who have identified with Freud's side in his quarrels, however, even Adler has been outranked by Jung, who is viewed as a particularly odious figure. Jung's opportunistic collaboration with the Nazis only put the final seal of disapproval on a man Freud's pupils had already learned to detest.

Nevertheless, here again the Tausk story will make more humanly plausible the motives behind the major controversies in Freud's life. In Tausk's suicide note he greeted not the Vienna Society, but the Psychoanalytic Association. For in 1910 Freud had founded an international association of psychoanalysts, with Jung as the president, and this had precipitated the fight with Adler. After having been so displeased with his Viennese pupils, Freud had finally found a worthy successor in Jung, a Swiss. Freud's "face beamed whenever he spoke of Jung: 'This is my beloved son, in whom I am well pleased.' "[8] Freud felt constricted by his milieu, and sought a wider environment for his work.

As a person Jung was far more striking than Adler. Freud made Adler president of the Vienna Society to soothe the hurt feelings of his Viennese followers, but instead this had only helped to mobilize Adler's independence. Adler was even-tempered, gregarious and sociable, but Jung possessed a really first-class mind. Freud very much wanted to hold Jung, who was a representative of academic psychiatry and came from a famous university clinic in Switzerland. For Freud, Jung represented the broader world of European science.

Jung had "an artistic personality, charming and beaming in his vitality, vague and whimsical in his formulations. . . ."[9] One could not imagine a man more different from Freud. As Freud wrote Jung, "I have invariably found that something in my personality, my words and ideas strike people as alien, whereas to you all hearts are open."[10]

As some years later Helene Deutsch quit her psychiatric post for the sake of practicing psychoanalysis and pleasing Freud, so too Jung departed from his university clinic. Jung's loyalty to Freud seemed unbounded. Jung was an extremely tall man, like Tausk much larger than Freud; and Freud was sensitive about his height. In a famous group photograph of analysts meeting in 1911, Jung can be seen crouching forward next to Freud. Mounted on a box, the master stands out as the leader of his group.*[11]

The same issue of priorities played its part in Freud's

* In later years Jung was assailed by Freud's students for his timidity in shying away from Freud's theory of infantile sexuality, and for watering down Freud's ideas to gain popularity. In fact Jung lived a far less sexually restricted life than Freud. Although a married man, Jung for many years had an affair with a psychiatrist and former patient of his, Antonia Wolff. Curiously enough, she plays no role in Jung's autobiography, although the pupils closest to him all attest the central part she played in his life.

break with Jung. Freud began to get upset at Swiss articles on psychoanalysis appearing "without mentioning his name."[12] Freud did not take being slighted lightly. He claimed that Jung had not quoted him as being the first to mention some ideas.[13] Jung, on his side, felt the same pressures that Tausk later experienced. A letter of Freud's alludes to Jung's objections: "Your reproach that I abuse psychoanalysis for the purpose of keeping my pupils in infantile dependency and that I myself am responsible for their infantile behaviour towards me. . . ."[14]

Freud and Jung each thought they were geniuses obstructed by the other. So Jung became "useless"[15] to Freud, and Freud put an end to the relationship. (Tausk again loyally backed Freud.) Freud wrote a tract against Adler and Jung, making sure that no one would confuse his own teachings with their "deviations"; each of their systems of thought, Freud complained, "takes hold of one fragment out of the wealth of themes in psychoanalysis and makes itself independent on the basis of this seizure. . . ."[16] Freud thus repudiated what seemed to him a "cool act of usurpation."[17]

Jung would have gone on with Freud, but as a loyal follower of Freud put it, "in his writing [Freud] never blotted out a line. . . . [H]e cancelled the whole thing and started to re-write it. . . . He always hated to patch up things, whether in the intellectual or emotional sphere."[18] Jung, in Freud's view, oversimplified matters, was "crazy,"[19] and his work was marred by "confusion." Although, as with Adler, Freud had done his best to expel

Jung, it seemed to the master that these two pupils, who took other analysts with them, had led "secessions" from psychoanalysis.

Freud was justified, to be sure, in worrying lest his original findings get lost in the theoretical tendencies Adler and Jung represented. Freud had found that sexuality develops in separate stages, and does not start with puberty; his great contribution to psychology lay in pointing to the persistence of infantile patterns in adult life.

From Freud's point of view Adler and Jung were endangering everything he had worked on. Adler and Jung would have shifted the focus away from what had been most distinctive in Freud's own work. It was by no means clear in those early days that these findings of Freud would one day be widely accepted—at which later time Adler's and Jung's concepts might provide a much-needed corrective.

Psychoanalytic knowledge was then confined to such a small group of people that Freud might understandably fear that it would get watered down before it had made its mark. The organization he headed was not yet large enough to permit much range of opinion. Lenin before the revolution faced a similar situation. So Freud had to fight more bitterly against backsliders than against the outside world, lest psychoanalysis get hopelessly confused with other techniques and theories. We do not need to doubt that "Freud put all the fire and vigour of his nature into answering . . . Adler and Jung. He never tired of finding new arguments against them, was always ready to return to the fray, and made his disciples join the fight."[20]

No one knew better than Freud how much he had meant to his followers, nor resented with more justice the way his own work lay, often unacknowledged, behind theirs. Freud's greatness as a teacher lay in his capacity to make demands, in his expectations for all his followers. Once Freud could count on absolute loyalty, he would do everything in his power to help. He could be kind and generous, supportive and encouraging, and his inspiration lifted this whole group of people beyond their previous attainments. Little wonder, then, if his pupils safeguarded their duties and commitments by idealizing him, if only to make it all seem worthwhile.

No matter how important it may be now to underline the ways in which they could be damaged by their relation to Freud, we should at the same time emphasize the extent to which he drew out of his pupils the strength they used in following him. A great teacher can release energies, allowing his students to go ahead on their own. As a model, Freud freed the aspirations of his followers. He made them better than they were.

Having been generous and outgoing with Adler and Jung, welcoming them into the world he was creating, Freud then drew back in bitterness and disappointment. These two disciples began that revolutionary tradition in psychoanalysis which all later figures in the movement have been both tempted and frightened by. Federn evaded rebellion one way, and Tausk another.

In the course of all Freud's hard work, as a clinician and a writer, he found himself in a whole series of human messes. The tangle with Tausk was only part and parcel of the others. Some pupils of Freud were able to resolve in a fulfilling way the same core conflicts that consumed Tausk. Yet these quarrels presupposed human greatness on Freud's part. In reflecting on these disputes it is easy to overlook one pervasive aspect—Freud's genius. It took a man of the greatest originality to attract all these people, and if some of them plunged to their destruction, Freud's life becomes the more humanly compelling and loses none of its historical significance.

2   *T*ausk's story not only provides a new slant on these famous public quarrels in Freud's career, but it also leads us into the center of all Freud's work. To begin with, the problem of telepathy had fascinated as well as repelled Freud for many years. Not only Freud, but also his closest followers, wrote about wordless communication. "If I were at the beginning rather than at the end of a scientific career, as I am today," Freud wrote in 1921, "I might possibly choose just this field of research [telepathy], in spite of all the difficulties."[21]

This nonrational side of Freud has often bothered people who prefer to see him simply as the cold scientist. Freud could be gullible about telepathy, even investigating telepathic seances. He was no believer in communicating with the dead, or in anyone's having real prophetic powers, but he did come to believe in "thought-transference." Whenever he wrote about telepathy, he invariably narrowed the problem down to the communication of thoughts without the mediation of conscious processes.

As a therapist, of course, the source of empathic understanding would interest him. But Freud always feared that his own belief in thought-transference would damage psychoanalysis in the eyes of the scientific world. He frequently warned his followers to be cautious about this subject, lest they tumble into mysticism. One of his own essays on telepathy was withheld from publication until after his death.

At times Freud protested his impartiality about telepathy. Yet he retained the feeling that with the subject of telepathy he might be about to make another discovery comparable to that of the meaningfulness of dream life. "They have both experienced the same contemptuous and arrogant treatment by official science."[22] Freud cherished the notion of his proclaiming "a conviction without taking into account any echo from the outer world."[23]

Freud had put Tausk off, he told Helene Deutsch, because Tausk's presence made an "uncanny" impression on him, due to his fears of Tausk's stealing his ideas. Lou once reported a "long conversation (in confidence)" with Freud "on those rare instances of thought-transference which certainly torment him."[24] In prophesying Tausk's lack of independence, Lou's imagery is curiously reminiscent and suggestive: "as if by a thought-transference he will always be busy with the same thing as Freud."

It might in fact be hard to distinguish the disagreeably "uncanny" feeling Freud had in Tausk's presence from the "torment" Freud felt about the more general issue of thought-transference. The theme of occultism, Freud said, "always discomposed" him.[25] When his pupils presented him with a medallion for his fiftieth birthday, the inscription on it turned out to be identical to the words Freud had, years before, fantasied for his own bust at the University of Vienna.* According to Jones's account, "when Freud read the inscription he became pale and agitated and in a strangled voice demanded to know who had thought of it."[26]

Freud could be downright superstitious. He admitted a belief in the magic of numbers.[27] We have already mentioned how he was plagued by the expectation that he would die at a certain date. But Freud also had the self-control to set out to explain the psychology of superstition, which at the very least should help us to understand his own problem: in people of "high intelligence," Freud wrote,

superstition is in large part the expectation of trouble; and a person who has harboured frequent evil wishes against others, but has been brought up to be good and has therefore repressed such wishes into the unconscious, will be especially ready to

* A line from Sophocles' *Oedipus Tyrannus:* "Who divined the famed riddle [of the Sphinx] and was a man most mighty."

expect punishment for his unconscious wickedness in the form
of trouble threatening from without.[28]

It is worthwhile to apply this suggestion of Freud's to
himself, in attempting to untangle his own superstitious
inclinations, and in particular his belief in thought-transference. As an aggressive man, whose ill will toward
others would conflict with an exceptionally severe conscience, Freud might uneasily fancy some retribution for
his own inner wrath. For Freud to expect to be repaid for
hostile wishes with some form of real disaster amounted,
of course, to an overestimation of the importance of the
power of his wishes, and of inner reality in general. Since,
furthermore, Freud believed that telepathic intimations
(thought-transferences) mainly presaged death or the possibility of death, it becomes possible to explain his particular belief in telepathy in terms of his own theory about
superstition in general.*

Freud's conviction about telepathy, the nature of his
superstitions, his fear of others stealing his ideas, his own
difficulties in remembering his sources, along with his
general overestimation of psychic reality—all this was of
a piece. And having come this far, it is only a short step
further to understanding how Freud's discoveries reflect
his own personality. The beginning of psychoanalysis, and

---

* Freud would probably have disagreed with this line of reasoning being
applied to himself, since he wrote that "my own superstition has its roots in
suppressed ambition (immortality). . . ."[29]

its most distinctive contribution to intellectual history, is marked by Freud's discovery that his patients' problems stemmed from inner, unconscious sources, and not just from common-sense, objective difficulties. It seems peculiarly fitting for a man who so overemphasized the power of his fantasies to have stressed the importance of the psychological dimension in life.

The technique of free associations also reveals a great deal about Freud's personality. He chose to spend his therapeutic time listening to the thoughts of his patients, inventing the technique of sitting out of their sight, behind the famed analytic couch. In the light of Freud's peculiar interests and anxieties, we can easily see how advantageous for him such an arrangement would be. No one need know his thoughts until he chose to reveal them through interpretations. The analyst helped the patient "by the offer of anticipatory ideas."[30] Meanwhile Freud could know the thoughts of others, every single piece in the flow of associations.

For Freud found out that if two apparently random ideas appear close together there must be some hidden inner connection between them. No matter how close Freud may have been at times to mysticism, in the end the scientist won out. Freud refused to accept the possibility of coincidence in psychic life. Some inner causation had to be behind every slip, dream, or symptom, and Freud set out to explain it rationally.

Alongside all of Freud's interest in the magical went an even more powerful strain of rationalism. Freud relied on the power of words for therapeutic cure. He was so threatened by the irrational that he could not allow himself to enjoy experiences in which lesser men have found release. Music positively irritated him, and he scarcely ever touched alcohol; he wrote about his inability to comprehend emotions like "transience" or the "oceanic feeling."

Intellectual control mattered so much to Freud that at times he even repudiated the existence of intuition.

[T]here are no sources of knowledge of the universe other than the intellectual working-over of carefully scrutinized observations. . . . [A]nd alongside of it no knowledge derived from revelation, intuition, or divination. . . . Intuition and divination . . . may safely be reckoned as illusions, the fulfillments of wishful impulses.[31]

The much-vaunted role of intuition in psychological understanding seemed to Freud a form of hocus-pocus; to the degree to which he recognized its existence at all, however, intuition was the result of rational self-control rather than of any emotional richness. "From what I have seen of intuition, it seems to me to be the product of a kind of intellectual impartiality."[32] To repudiate intuition while accepting telepathy seems starkly inconsistent. Yet if Freud sometimes had to emphasize the rational so much, it was only because the irrational was so strong in him.

*3   T*he story of Freud's conflict with Tausk has so far helped to illuminate some of the personal sources of Freud's discoveries, and to make his controversies with his followers and predecessors more comprehensible. Further elucidation of the differences between Freud and Tausk can help reveal what sort of therapist Freud actually was, and wherein lay Tausk's distinctive contribution to psychotherapy.

Although in his obituary Freud downplayed Tausk's clinical experience, Tausk's enduring contribution has been to psychiatry, not to the philosophic foundations of psychoanalysis. As discussed earlier, Tausk's training with hospitalized cases set him apart from other psychoanalysts of his day. Jung before Tausk and Harry Stack Sullivan after Tausk's death both led the application of psychoanalytic concepts to the treatment of psychosis. But for his time and among Freud's loyal followers, Tausk pioneered in using Freud's ideas to understand psychosis. Within Freud's school Tausk's contributions laid the basis for future workers; both Bruno Bettelheim and Erik Erikson have been indebted to Tausk's innovations.

Even today the distinction between psychosis (the province of the old-fashioned psychiatrist) and neurosis (the area of Freud's psychoanalysis) is not by any means a settled matter. The more a therapist is interested in the dynamics or treatment of a case, the more likely he would be nowadays to label it "neurotic." A diagnosis of psychosis still has chilling therapeutic implications. In purely practical terms, a psychosis can be considered the outcome of a patient's inability to handle his neurosis. The difference between being neurotic and being psychotic is the same as the distinction between having a hang-up, or the hang-up having you.

A neurotic has trouble understanding his inner world, whereas a psychotic has difficulty testing external reality. A schizophrenic, for example, with so few human ties, finds his loneliness so close to death that he is therefore forced to create his own world. The psychotic not only withdraws from the outside world, but also struggles to get back in contact with it through delusions or hallucinations.

In Tausk's time psychosis was not at all a subtle diagnosis; it simply meant the patient was crazy. Psychiatrists working with such gross disorders had very little coherent understanding of what they treated. As a consolidated science, psychiatry was then relatively new, and its approach rested on an organic orientation.

The personality of the mentally sick person was not considered as a subject of any particular interest; furthermore it was not believed that the psychotic manifestations could be expressions of the personality. . . . The symptomatology of psychoses was considered the result of the disturbance of the mosaic of brain functions and brain cells, comparable to the effect of sitting down by chance on the keyboard of a piano and thereby provoking a senseless noise.[33]

Psychoanalysis at least established that psychosis was not a "senseless conglomeration of symptoms unrelated to personality."[34]

Not sharing today's emphasis on treatment, psychiatrists then were concerned more with the custodial care of psychotics. The world had to be protected from them, and they from the world. Even though psychiatrists lacked psychological explanations for their patient's troubles, they were superb at describing psychiatric syndromes. Psychoanalysis, by its emphasis on the meaningfulness of symptoms, ultimately increased the humaneness with which these patients were handled. Yet the scientific interest of early analysts in the psychology of these cases was often accompanied by a lack of concern with the possibilities of cure.

Everything can depend on the personality of the psychiatrist. In a sense, these old-time psychiatrists did not "know" enough to realize they could not do what they in fact sometimes accomplished. Wagner-Jauregg, for example, had a deep, quieting voice that had a great therapeutic impact. Rude though he could be in externals, he cared about his patients. These psychiatrists were sometimes able to help their patients with symptomatic remedies, even though they might not have been able to explain why they had their successes.

Freud's own attitude toward psychosis is no easy matter to untangle, since like others he took so long in distinguishing between neurosis and psychosis. In 1904, for example, he wrote:

I have been able to elaborate and to test my therapeutic method only on severe, indeed on the severest cases; at first my material consisted entirely of patients who had tried everything else without success, and had spent long years in sanatoria. . . . Psychoanalytic therapy was created through and for the treatment of patients permanently unfit for existence, and its triumph has been that it has made a satisfactorily large number of these permanently fit for existence.[35]

Yet Freud did not mean to include the psychoses within the category of the "severest cases." The people he treated were either not as sick as he liked to think, or much sicker than he was then aware. However, Freud did hope that through suitable changes in technique psychotic processes might in the future be treatable.

In these early days Freud did not show much interest in distinguishing between neurosis and psychosis; they were "not separated by a hard and fast line"[36] in his mind, any more than health and illness were sharply distinguished from each other. Freud sought to extend psychoanalytic influence wherever he could. However, insofar as he did differentiate between neurosis and psychosis, Freud felt that the difficulty in treating a psychotic lay in his indifference to the therapist. Because of the psychotic patient's excess of self-involvement, his narcissism, he could not develop a transference.

What cures, Freud thought, is the capacity of a person

to get beyond himself, to maintain distance toward his own feelings. Without this distancing, a therapeutic alliance between patient and analyst becomes impossible. As late as 1937 Freud's considered opinion remained that since this cooperation was impossible with psychotic patients, their psychological treatment was out of the question.[37] By very different reasoning, Freud had adopted the view of old-fashioned academic psychiatry that psychotics were untreatable.

But one crucial question remains—which disturbances are to be considered neurotic and which psychotic? In Tausk's time Freud considered dementia praecox, what we now more commonly call schizophrenia, a "narcissistic neurosis."[38] By labeling this illness a "neurotic disorder," Freud was underlining the notion that psychoanalysis could help to understand these cases and in the future make them accessible to treatment. Until forced to clarify the distinction between neurosis and psychosis, Freud worked as if his treatment was applicable "to an unlimited number of patients."[39] The early psychoanalysts did savor the notion of putting everyone into analysis. Not until the 1920's did Freud place "narcissistic neurosis" under the heading of psychosis. In other words, in Tausk's era Freud was using the term neurosis as an enormous wastebasket, encompassing cases that later on would be clearly differentiated from garden-variety neurotics.

The purpose of this digression into the history of psychoanalytic terminology is to indicate that Freud was interested in the psychoses as a scientist, but not as a therapist.

He even maintained that "the analytic study of the psychoses is impracticable owing to its lack of therapeutic results."[40] Yet he was interested in what other workers had been able to find out.

It is widely known among Freud's pupils, if not among the public at large, that Freud himself had very little psychiatric experience. His own research before founding psychoanalysis had been in neurology. Although as a neurologist, and even sometimes in private psychoanalytic practice, he could not help coming across cases of psychosis, he steered clear of psychotics whenever he could. He certainly never identified himself with academic psychiatry in any way. To a Swiss pupil who tried to mediate between psychiatry and psychoanalysis, Freud wrote in 1911: "I really look upon your expectation as heretical."[41]

In his discussion of primary process thinking in *The Interpretation of Dreams,* Freud had pointed out many dream mechanisms that appear in psychosis, and had declared that the dream itself was a normal prototype of psychotic experience. But beyond this attempt at an abstract understanding of psychosis, Freud was not interested in comprehending clinical psychiatric entities or configurations. As Tausk pointed out, Freud's "piece-meal method of investigation does not lead to an over-all picture of the individual."[42] When a case was not one of the classical neuroses, either obsessional or hysteric, Freud would have trouble establishing a diagnosis.

Freud sometimes treated cases psychoanalytically, as if

they were neurotics, when it later turned out that much more serious psychiatric trouble underlay a mere façade of neurosis. Freud saw psychotics when he took them as patients without realizing the severity of their illness. For example, he sometimes cured a neurotic symptom, only for the patient to fall back on an underlying psychosis.* As Freud once wrote to a distressed pupil, "you have had the bad luck to run into a latent paranoia, and through the cure of his neurosis you may have freed the way for a more serious sickness. That happens to each of us occasionally and there is no protection against it."[43]

Diagnosing a psychosis, then as well as now, can be a very difficult matter. Like others, Tausk was capable of making exactly such a mistake. But Freud wanted to keep away from the whole problem of psychosis. He was interested in more refined mental suffering. Anyone who could make his way punctually to analytic treatment six times a week in the midst of a busy city had to be in good contact with reality. Freud did write one case history about a psychotic, but he never saw this man as a patient, describing his illness instead on the basis of a book of memoirs.

Freud reacted to psychotics with the defensiveness shared by most people. He wanted to keep his distance, to avoid them. In Freud's time psychosis was even more incom-

---

* In one such case, where the original symptom had been agoraphobia (fear of open spaces), Freud had had to reintroduce the agoraphobia through hypnosis in order to undo the damage of the treatment.[44]

prehensible than it is today. Many have hypothesized that these illnesses are chemical or biological processes, expressing themselves psychologically. But Freud was more than usually standoffish about psychotics. They were so incomprehensible as to seem "uncanny" to him.[45] Thus he would, for example, have had relatively little experience with suicides, since a suicidal patient would be too great a risk for an analysis. Freud's intolerance of mental illness would be considered unacceptable in a therapist today.

Freud was not an old-fashioned physician with a need to cure. He was no lover of mankind. He wrote of his "disappointment in human beings."[46] The older Freud became, the more what he called his "indifference to the world" came out. "In the depths of my heart I can't help being convinced that my dear fellowmen, with a few exceptions, are worthless."[47] ". . . I have found little that is 'good' about human beings on the whole. In my experience most of them are trash."[48] "I have never done anything mean or malicious and cannot trace any temptation to do so. . . ." But "other people are brutal and untrustworthy."[49]

Freud considered himself an observer and a discoverer —not a healer. He claimed to have no predilection for a career as a physician, and lacked, as he put it, "a genuine medical temperament"; "I became a therapist against my will."[50] Freud's scientific side produced his great achievement, that body of ideas which other workers have been able to develop and change.

Psychoanalysis mattered more to Freud for its possibilities of research than for its therapeutic effectiveness. Of course Freud's patients could mean very much to him personally, and he could be very active, even manipulative, in his treatment. Especially in his earlier years, Freud could be outgoing in his therapeutic efforts. Many patients have reported Freud's warmth and humanity, the good human contact he had with them and how interested he could be.

But any supportive moves were distinct in Freud's mind from analysis, and he always feared that the scientific part of his work would get swallowed up in therapy. As Freud aged, he grew increasingly skeptical of the earlier cures he thought he had accomplished; he became more distant from human contact in general and more devoted to the goal of pure research. As he turned away from medicine, Freud repeatedly warned against the danger of turning psychoanalysis into a "mere handmaid of psychiatry." Freud wanted a separate profession of psychoanalysts, not necessarily doctors, who would devote themselves to the pursuit of scientific knowledge. Problems like relieving suffering, prevention, and cure would solve themselves, he thought, provided only that we learn enough about the nature of the forces at work.

In ruling psychotics out of bounds for psychoanalytic treatment, Freud grouped them with delinquents, addicts, and perverts—none of whom were "worthy" of an analysis. As he once wrote, "regretfully, only a few patients are worth the trouble we spend on them, so that we are not allowed to have a therapeutic attitude but we must be

glad to have learned something in every case."[51] Or again,
"it would be uneconomical to squander such expenditure
[of psychoanalysis] upon completely worthless persons
who happen to be neurotic."[52] Intellectually intrepid and
bent on making discoveries, Freud did not want to have
to moralize. If patients were to fulfill themselves without
having to be told how to live, then Freud had to presup-
pose that they already possessed a self.

Freud's preference was for the strong, not the weak.
The truthfulness of the patient was to be reciprocated by
the analyst's honesty. His method of treatment assumed
patients had considerable mental self-discipline and capacity for integrating their newly won insights. He com-
plimented a patient at the end of a three months' analysis
in 1907, "What I liked best was that as soon as you understood something you could make use of it."[53] Psychoanalysis meant pulling problems apart, on the assumption
patients were self-sufficient enough to know best how to
put things together. As Freud once wrote, "psychoanalysis
meets the optimum of favorable conditions where its practice is not needed—i.e., among the healthy."[54]

4   *F*reud demanded that people grow up; he wanted
the best out of people, and expected more of mankind.
His therapy was based on the notion that people can
change, and overcome themselves. Freud said No—to dis-

honesty, ignorance, stupidity, symptoms, self-deceptions, suffering, but also to weakness, dependencies, support, tolerance, acceptingness.

The most painful emotional conflicts can arise precisely when someone is unable to make use of whatever insight he has. It would be inhuman for an analyst to wait for the effects of rationality while patients are bearing terrible suffering. More may be needed in therapy than just a teacher. The task of the therapist may be not to expose more material from the depths, but to shore up a weak ego. Tausk pointed to the importance of what we now call "ego psychology," in neurosis as well as psychosis, as early as anyone in Freud's circle. According to Lou, "while Tausk's concept of neurosis . . . is the same as Freud's, he emphasized the 'failure' in the sphere of the ego, and hence in the social sphere, as an absolutely necessary condition for the outbreak of neurosis."[55]

Tausk was far more willing than Freud to approach psychotics and to learn from them. As a therapist he was less austere, more accepting of human weakness, more able to identify with a patient and care for him. While Freud strove to make people better than they were by giving them the tools for self-understanding, Tausk was more inclined to help people accept themselves. In one case of male homosexuality, Tausk was more understanding than Freud would have been able to be. In this instance Tausk saw that the patient had so few heterosexual traces that he had to be helped to accept his deviation and to free himself from guilt feelings.[56]

Freud himself would have had to struggle against his

own defensive repugnance toward such a person. For his time Freud was tolerant, and he wanted to understand the roots of perversion, but he found it easier to condemn such a person than to help. About one male homosexual case, Freud commented that "if worst comes to worst, one ships such people . . . across the ocean with some money, let us say to South America, and lets them there seek and find their destiny." Of another case he expressed a similar distaste: Freud considered the patient "obviously a scoundrel who is not worth your trouble." Freud contrasted this case to another who "is obviously a worth-while human being and deserves to be treated. . . ."[57]

Side by side with all Freud's moralism, he could at times be extraordinarily pragmatic. Masturbatory fantasies in intercourse were all right, as long as they helped heterosexual potency. Female homosexuality bothered Freud little; in one case of a depressed middle-aged woman, Freud considered her transformation into an active Lesbian, without guilt, a successful outcome of her psychoanalysis. Freud certainly disliked goody-goodies, and in what he considered a "worthy" person he would put up with much that would otherwise offend him. Freud always distinguished between health and worth—"There are 'healthy' people who are not worth anything, and on the other hand 'unhealthy' neurotic people who are very worthy individuals indeed."[58]

Tausk represented a broadening of therapeutic interests for psychoanalysis. Like Adler and Jung, and each of the dissenters within classical psychoanalysis in future decades (e.g., Otto Rank and Sandor Ferenczi), Tausk wanted to extend the areas of psychotherapeutic treatment. Only with the development of ego psychology within psychoanalysis did adaptations in the scope of treatment beyond the classical neuroses become possible. Freud had at first held the view that to make something conscious can only be to weaken it.[59] But removing self-deceptions presupposes that the patient's ego is capable of integrating the new insight presented to it. Otherwise, psychoanalysis may simply strip away a patient's defenses, leaving him sicker than he ever was.

Tausk and his friend Federn were more compassionate about illness, and instead of labeling psychotics as narcissistic—being too self-involved—Tausk saw them as suffering from a deficiency in ego strength. The psychotic's problem, then, was weakness rather than excess. Tausk felt that if a therapist could lend some strength to the psychotic's ego, his ability to distinguish between his self and the outside world would return. The boundaries of the ego could then expand, and the patient could better separate inner feelings from outer realities. This notion of ego boundaries was Tausk's original formulation[60] and it was designed to emphasize that ego defects lay behind schizophrenia.

In this view the psychotic's organizing ability was weak. The therapist had to come to the rescue of the psychotic's ego, to help it master its unruly instinctual drives. Neither Tausk nor Federn would have denied the practical difficulties of such treatment. If you arouse the involvement of a psychotic in the outside world, when he is already suffering from a weak ego, then you may force him to withdraw even further as he exhausts his limited capacities. The analytic method, Tausk thought, needed to be changed to make these patients accessible to treatment. But there was no longer a theoretical reason for excluding them from the psychoanalyst's purview, nor for excluding all the other cases deemed by Freud "unworthy" of treatment. After Tausk's death, Federn was responsible for developing these ideas within Freud's circle.[61]

The study of ego psychology began under Tausk and Federn with the treatment of psychotic disorders. Subsequently other analysts, like Anna Freud, became interested in the treatment of children, and made notable contributions in systematizing ego psychology. Erik Erikson, originally a student of Anna Freud's, has made famous the concept of "ego identity." Recently Erikson referred to Federn's concept of "ego boundaries" as having been "much discussed" while he was in training at the Vienna Psychoanalytic Society in the late twenties.[62] But as Federn privately admitted, the concept of ego boundaries had really been originated by Victor Tausk. (One can only wonder if Federn's reluctance in later years to acknowledge Tausk's contribution may not have in part reflected his shock at the circumstances surrounding Tausk's untimely death.) And the concept of "identity" itself was first introduced into the psychoanalytic literature by Tausk, in his paper on the "influencing machine."[63]

Although Freud himself considered therapeutic work with psychotic patients futile, in later years he did not order Federn to stop trying with such cases; he simply did not want to participate in the work himself. As with Tausk earlier, Freud found Federn's formulations unintelligible. But Freud still sent Federn cases and never tried to drive him out of his circle.

Although he was capable of being very aggressive to colleagues, as a man Federn was warm and amiable, even a trifle fatuous. Famous for his slips of the tongue, he had the kind of fluid personality that offered patients non-verbal means of support. According to an old Viennese adage, only a good man can be a good physician. Federn would "fight harder against greater odds to help the patient than Freud in whom the scientist was always stronger than the healer."[64] But in therapy, "the scientific method is not always the best for illuminating a personality," Tausk once maintained; "art is often better suited for that purpose."[65]

Federn reacted to one patient by stressing "the likeable impression" that the man created, while Freud thought the same person was "an absolute swine."[66] Freud was very sensitive to the "resistances" patients threw up to treatment, and he recurred to battle images to describe a therapeutic encounter. In Freud's view an analysis involved a superior and a subordinate; the patient "submitted" to an analysis. Freud always stressed the danger of too much therapeutic zeal in the analyst, and warned against it again and again.

Less able to accept the maternal in himself, Freud

thought that above all an analyst must be aware of what he does. As long as he acted in the patient's interests, and not out of the need for some personal gratification, Freud would countenance a good deal of activity on the analyst's part. But an analyst who gives more of himself necessarily exposes the patient to greater disappointment and loss. The analyst's neutrality may block spontaneity, but distance may also protect the patient from the analyst's sadism. Of course passivity in the analyst, as we have now learned, can be in itself aggressive. But Freud was wary of the ethics of suggestive therapy. He did not like deceit or coercion: "the patient should be educated to liberate and fulfill his own nature, not to resemble ourselves."[67]

After Tausk's death, when Federn became the representative within the Vienna Society of the trend in therapy most opposed to Freud's own approach, he paid a price for his eagerness not to be lured into being another Jung or Adler, or even a Tausk. He kept his concepts ambiguous and unclarified lest his divergence from Freud's own notions become, especially to himself, too apparent. Much less of a scientific investigator to begin with, Federn was in such conflict that it handicapped his writing, and his concepts became clear-cut only long after Freud's death.

We now know that difficulties in treating psychotics do not stem, as Freud had thought, from their inability to "transfer" emotions. Sometimes they become involved too readily and too intensely, and for this reason it is not easy to establish a working relationship with them. Schizophrenics, for example, are acutely sensitive to whether they are being accepted or not. And their hostile, angry feelings often interfere with treatment. Even loving indulgence on the part of the therapist may not be enough; it may only mobilize the patient's guilt feelings and make him withdraw even further.

Tausk's great ambition was to find a way of understanding and treating those mysterious disorders which are called psychoses. Freud's own lack of interest in psychoses permitted Tausk to last as long as he did within Freud's world. With much more distance than Federn, Tausk wanted to solve the problem of the great mental illnesses. When we realize how even today psychiatrists are groping around in this field, classifying wherever they still lack understanding, we begin to see the immense scope of Tausk's ambitions.

Tausk presented a paper on melancholia before the Vienna Society on December 30, 1914. During the discussion on Tausk's paper Freud first publicly expressed his views on manic-depressive problems. (Unlike schizophrenics, the other great group of psychotics, manic-depressives do not tend to end in deterioration.) Shortly thereafter, in February 1915, Freud wrote a first draft of a classic paper called "Mourning and Melancholia." Yet he did not publish it for two years. The war delayed the publication of much psychoanalytic material, but in this case it was mainly that Freud wanted to ruminate over his essay.

Tausk, as we have seen, worked quite differently. In a

lecture on the war psychoses, delivered in January 1916 in Lublin, Tausk included a complete review of Freud's concepts on melancholia. He repeatedly referred to "verbal remarks" of Freud's. At one point he mentioned "a still unpublished conjecture of Freud's (which I quote here with his special permission). . . ."[68] We can understand why Freud had to be cautious with this man; in addition to his having ideas of his own, he would rush ahead to fill out some of Freud's raw concepts with his own clinical material.

Tausk had a great need to be creative; as he remarked at one point in this paper, "it would be easy to become famous by laying claim to the discovery of a new psychosis. . . ."[69] Yet Tausk's paper, which is historically important since he was working on melancholia simultaneously with Freud, was damaged by his competitiveness. Tausk could not simply accept his own originality. He spoiled his discussion by going into too many details of Freud's views, and he burdened his argument with references to Freud's comments. At the very end of his paper Tausk inserted a footnote criticizing a psychiatrist for writing without mentioning Freud's name.

But when Freud's paper finally appeared in 1917, a year after Tausk's, Freud did not quote or cite Tausk's work on melancholia at all, and consequently Freud's pupils have ignored it. Of course Freud had privately pondered over the problem for years. But he did cite other contemporary writers, and in all fairness Tausk deserved mention as one of the few psychoanalysts then working on the problem. The matter of footnoting was no scholastic issue in that circle, and Freud knew it. "We knew these books [of Freud's] by heart, including all the footnotes. . . ."[70] Freud did cite Tausk in that essay on melancholia, but not in the right place—not for Tausk's work on melancholia.*

The paper that earned Tausk the greatest psychiatric fame discussed the symptom of the "influencing machine" in schizophrenia. Tausk read the paper before the Vienna Society on January 6, 1918, and another evening of the Society was devoted to it on January 30, 1918; a year later it appeared in print.

In this paper Tausk developed the concept of projection in a clinical psychiatric context. Freud had postulated that psychosis involved a regression of libido back to primary narcissism; the most primitive stage of child development involves concentrating on one's own body. Tausk showed how schizophrenic symptoms can represent the earliest stages of the ego's contact with reality. Feelings of inner strangeness get projected onto the external world. Changes

* According to Jones, "Whereas in his neurological work Freud's bibliographical references had been scrupulously exact and comprehensive, when it came to his analytical writings this was no longer so. Rank once jokingly remarked that Freud distributed references to other analysts' writings on the same principle as the Emperor distributed decorations, according to the mood and fancy of the moment. More than that, he would redistribute them. I remember his attributing an important conclusion of mine in a book he had read to the reviewer of the book; but then at the moment I was out of favor and he was in."[71]

in one's own personality are experienced as coming from the outside world.

Tausk interpreted the common schizophrenic delusion of being influenced by machines in a persecutory way as an externalized representation of the patient's own body. The influencing machine, then, is a projection of the patient's body, as a defense against regressing to primary narcissism. Extending his clinical insight, Tausk went on to comment that "machines produced by man's ingenuity and created in the image of man are unconscious projections of man's bodily structure."[72]

Here Freud conceded that Tausk was ahead of him. Freud used Tausk's case material (as Tausk later duly noted) in a paper he wrote in the spring of 1915. Freud commented, briefly, "Dr. Victor Tausk . . . has placed at my disposal some observations that he has made in the initial stages of schizophrenia. . . ."[73] In Tausk's paper, which did not appear until 1919, he falls all over himself making acknowledgments to others. At one point Tausk mentions Freud's earlier work on schizophrenia, and twice he acknowledges Freud's comments on the paper at the Vienna Society. He also cites twice, to make the noose even tighter, remarks of Helene Deutsch during the discussion of his paper.

Curiously enough, Kafka, who shared so many other similarities with Tausk, also wrote about the machine as a projection of the human body. His "In the Penal Colony" describes the same mechanism that Tausk had come across in his psychiatric work. In Kafka's tale, a machine controls thoughts and feelings as it drives punishment into the victim's body; finally, body and machine become stuck together.[74]

Tausk's writings ranged over so many different fields that he never fulfilled his great promise. He had defied Freud's advice to his pupils that one must concentrate on a single theme. In addition to his exploration of the manic-depressive and schizophrenia psychoses, Tausk had contributed to the understanding of ego psychology, artistic creativity, the philosophical underpinnings of psychoanalysis, as well as the relationship between law and psychiatry. With his one paper on the "influencing machine," Tausk won a pioneering place in the psychological understanding of schizophrenic delusions, and this work has been built upon by others—for example, by Bruno Bettelheim in his treatment of seriously disturbed children.[75] But Tausk died so early that his work now seems scattered.

Despite the limited psychiatric fame his achievements won, Tausk's suicide almost totally extinguished his memory in the world at large. After his death in 1919, Kosa Lazarević—with whom he lived in Belgrade during the war—came to Vienna to meet his sister Jelka; and every year thereafter Kosa journeyed to Vienna to care for the grave.

Tausk's two sons had little to do with the psychoanalytic community. Marius, who had earlier planned to become a psychiatrist, went through medical school but chose not to practice; in 1926 he attended a meeting of the Vienna Society, and Federn warmly greeted this son of his dead friend. Victor Hugo, the younger boy, was accepted by Hitschmann for an analysis free of charge between September of 1923 and February of 1924; the end of the analysis consisted of a visit to his father's grave in an effort to clear his mind of a haunting memory. Despite their broken family and the truly traumatic death of their father—the most important event, Freud thought, in a man's life—both sons managed well.

In the two decades between Tausk's death and Freud's own in 1939, Tausk's name came up only occasionally. Freud cited Tausk one more time, mentioned him casually in conversation now and then, but for all intents and purposes (with the exception of the "influencing machine" article) Tausk, his life and conflicts, had disappeared from the face of the earth.

Then in 1934 suddenly the whole story reappeared momentarily in print. Somehow one of Tausk's articles had escaped being destroyed with the rest of his papers. Tausk might never have permitted it to appear if he had lived. For at the very end of this paper, in a mere footnote, Tausk revealed the crux of his struggle with Freud. It was all so unknown that the publishers had no idea what the footnote referred to. The article was short, concerning a man called "B" who experiences a block in relation to a revered master, Ibsen. Tausk explains the situation within the jargon of psychoanalytic terminology current in his day. Yet it remains a succinct summary of his own quarrel with Freud.

B's relation to Ibsen, that of a creative individual to the master who represents his ideals, is patterned after the father complex. . . . In the life of rivals struggling with their masters, the hatred . . . is derived from the son-father relation. Hence the conflict between master and disciple striving for independence resembles very closely the severest type of conflict between father and son.[1]

Four years later, in 1938, the old guard around Freud had occasion once more to think of Tausk. The Nazis were driving Freud and his pupils from Vienna, and the analysts now in difficult financial straits had heard that Tausk's son Marius had done well as an endocrinologist and pharmacologist in Holland; so Federn got in touch with him to see if the loans to his father could now be repaid. Hitschmann, Jekels, Steiner, and Federn had, as mentioned earlier, all helped put Tausk through medical school. Once informed of the debts Marius did not hesitate to pay.

Federn also mentioned to Marius that Freud had been one of Tausk's creditors, so Marius wrote Freud to ask how much was owed him. Freud behaved like a correct gentleman. Though suffering from cancer of the jaw since 1923, and only a year away from his own death, this secluded invalid of eighty-two remained as formidable as ever; retaining all his sense of dignity and punctiliousness, Freud wrote back to say that he could not remember how much he had lent Marius's father, it could not have been much anyway, and it did not matter any more.

1938 was a terrible year for Europe, as World War II approached from every direction. A younger brother of Tausk's, Mirko, died fighting in Spain in January. And when the Nazis entered Vienna, Jelka, her husband Ernst, and her husband's brother Camillo found they were trapped. They had no money to live abroad, their health had begun to decline, and suddenly they felt old. Jelka wrote a farewell note to her old mother in Yugoslavia— "We have been so happy and do not want to be unhappy." And then the three of them, like so many others at that time, committed suicide. Victor's mother never recovered from the blow of their deaths, and died herself the same year.

Chronology
Notes
Acknowledgments
Index

CHRONOLOGY

1856	Sigmund Freud born in Freiberg, Moravia.
1879, March 12	Victor Tausk born in Zsilina, Slovakia.
1897	Tausk goes to study law at the University of Vienna.
1900	Freud publishes *The Interpretation of Dreams*.
1900	Tausk marries Martha Frisch, and they move to Yugoslavia.
1902	Tausk receives his doctorate in jurisprudence. Tausk's first son, Marius, born.
1903	Tausk's second son, Victor Hugo, born.
1905	Victor and Martha separate, and go to Vienna. Tausk writes "Husein Brko" and "Twilight."
1906	Tausk moves to Berlin and works as a journalist.
1907	Tausk spends twenty-five days in a sanatorium. Tausk meets Lea Rosen in Berlin.
1908, October	Tausk returns to Vienna. He and Martha officially divorce. Tausk begins to study medicine at the University of Vienna.

1909, October	Tausk first attends meetings of the Vienna Psychoanalytic Society.
1909, November 24	Tausk presents his first paper to Freud's group, "Theory of Knowledge and Psychoanalysis."
1911	Alfred Adler resigns from the Vienna Psychoanalytic Society.
1912	Tausk publishes a paper "On Masturbation." Helene Deutsch begins work at Wagner-Jauregg's clinic in Vienna.
1912–13	Lou Andreas-Salomé goes to Vienna, and she and Tausk have a love affair.
1913	Quarrel between Freud and Jung. Tausk publishes two papers, "A Contribution to the Psychology of Child-sexuality" and "Compensation as a Means of Discounting the Motive of Repression."
1914, June	Tausk completes his medical studies.
1915, August	Tausk called up as army psychiatrist.
1915	Tausk publishes a paper "On the Psychology of the Alcoholic Occupation Delirium."
1916, March 25	Tausk's father dies.
1916	Tausk publishes a paper "Diagnostic Considerations Concerning the Symptomatology of the So-called War-psychoses."
1916, December	Tausk transferred from Lublin to Belgrade. Tausk lives with Kosa Lazarević.
1917	Tausk delivers a paper "On the Psychology of the War Deserter."
1918, September	At the Budapest Congress of psychoanalysts, Tausk delivers a paper "Psychoanalysis and the Capacity for Judgment."
1918, November 4	Tausk returns to Vienna and resumes his psychoanalytic practice.

1918, December	Freud refuses to analyze Tausk, and sends him to Helene Deutsch (already in analysis with Freud).
1919, January	Tausk enters analysis with Helene Deutsch.
1919, March	Tausk's analysis terminated on Freud's initiative.
1919, Spring	Tausk becomes engaged to marry Hilde Loewi.
1919, July 3	Tausk commits suicide.
1919	Freud's obituary of Tausk appears, along with Tausk's paper "On the Origin of the 'influencing machine' in Schizophrenia."

choanalytic Society, eds. H. Nunberg and E. Federn (New York: International Universities Press; 1962), I, xxii–xxiii. Cf. also Edoardo Weiss: *The Structure and Dynamics of the Human Mind* (New York: Grune & Stratton; 1960), p. xvi. On occasion Tausk is credited with a specific clinical insight. Cf. Edoardo Weiss: "Emotional Memories and Acting Out," *Psychoanalytic Quarterly,* XI, 4 (1942), 485. Typically, Sandor Ferenczi regarded Tausk as "an analyst whose too early death we all deplore." *Further Contributions to the Theory and Technique of Psychoanalysis* (London: Hogarth Press; 1926), p. 369. Otto Rank mentioned the "valuable work of Tausk, who died prematurely." *The Trauma of Birth* (New York: Harcourt, Brace & Co.; 1929), p. 69. And at least one psychiatrist was "to no small degree attracted to psychoanalysis by Tausk's enthusiasm and by his brilliant presentation of the Freudian theory." Dorian Feigenbaum, in *Psychoanalytic Quarterly,* Vol. 2 (1933), p. 519. Enough exists in the memoirs of contemporaries to indicate the extent of Freud's confidence in Tausk. Over Wilhelm Stekel's objections, Freud once appointed Tausk to supervise the reviews to be published in the main psychoanalytic journal. Tausk and Stekel were enemies, and years later Freud sided with Tausk's judgment of Stekel. Cf. Stekel: *Autobiography,* ed. Emil Gutheil (New York: Liveright Publishing Co.; 1950), pp. 142–3. Ernest Jones: *The Life and Work of Sigmund Freud* (London: Hogarth Press; 1954), II, 136. Joseph Wortis: *Fragment of an Analysis with Freud* (New York: Charter Books; 1963), p. 163. From Ernest Jones's official biography of Freud one can glean some further bits of information. Jones mentions that after Adler's resignation from the Vienna Psychoanalytic Society in 1911 there were left "Stekel, Sadger and Tausk, all of whom gave Freud a deal of trouble." In writing about the "backbiting, acid remarks, quarrels over priority in small matters" within the Vienna Society, Jones lists Tausk among "the most troublesome in this respect." While discussing

Freud's "feminine side," and the way his dependent needs could lead him to overestimate some of his pupils, Jones illustrates these trends manifested "with Adler and Jung, and to some extent with Ferenczi, Silberer, and Tausk." Jones: *Life of Freud*, II, 86, 129, 420. Freud once referred a very important case to Tausk. Cf. Edward Glover: "David Eder," in *David Eder*, ed. J. G. Hobman (London: Gollancz; 1945), p. 98.

With the help of Lou's *Journal* and Freud's obituary, Tausk secured a five-page place in *Psychoanalytic Pioneers,* eds. Franz Alexander, Martin Grotjahn, and Samuel Eisenstein (New York: Basic Books; 1966), pp. 235–9. For some passing references to Tausk, cf. Vincent Brome: *Freud and His Early Circle* (London: Heinemann; 1967) and *Reich Speaks of Freud,* eds. Mary Higgins and Chester Raphael (New York: Farrar, Straus & Giroux; 1967).

5. Freud quotes Tausk's account of a secular Jewish upbringing, which was Tausk's own. Cf. "Psychopathology of Everyday Life," *Standard Edition*, Vol. 6, pp. 92–3.

6. Cf. ibid. for Tausk's baptism before marriage.

7. "An Autobiographical Study," *Standard Edition*, Vol. 20, p. 55. Also interview with Oliver Freud, April 22, 1966.

8. Quoted in Jones: *Life of Freud*, II, 71.

9. "On the History of the Psychoanalytic Movement," *Standard Edition*, Vol. 14, p. 26.

10. Cf. "Papers on Technique," *Standard Edition*, Vol. 12, pp. 85–171. In his "Introductory Lectures on Psychoanalysis" Freud wrote that "psychoanalysis is a procedure for the medical treatment of neurotic patients." *Standard Edition*, Vol. 15, p. 15. On the other hand, Freud wrote in 1913 as a preface for a layman's book that "the practice of psychoanalysis calls much less for medical training than for psychological instruction and a free human outlook." "Introduction to Pfister's *The Psychoanalytic Method*," *Standard Edition*, Vol. 12, pp. 330–1.

11. For example, Dr. Sandor Rado and Dr. Therese Benedek.

12. Fritz Wittels: *Sigmund Freud* (New York: Dodd Mead & Co.; 1924), p. 136.

13. Ludwig Binswanger: *Sigmund Freud* (New York: Grune & Stratton; 1957), pp. 5–6.

14. Heinz Hartmann: *Reminiscences* (Columbia Oral History Project), p. 4.

15. Lou may have altered her immediate impressions of that year in Vienna, changing entries in the light of later events. And it has been suggested that her literary executor may have made his own emendations. Rudolph Binion: *Frau Lou* (Princeton: Princeton University Press; 1968), p. 465.

16. Freud wrote a short paper about the meeting, "On Transience," *Standard Edition*, Vol. 14, p. 305.

17. Lou Andreas-Salomé: *The Freud Journal*, tr. Stanley A. Leavy (New York: Basic Books; 1964), p. 131.

18. "An Autobiographical Study," *Standard Edition*, Vol. 20, p. 72. 1912 was also a critical year in Freud's falling-out with Jung.

Chapter II

1. "Introductory Lectures on Psychoanalysis," *Standard Edition*, Vol. 16, p. 285.

2. *Letters of Sigmund Freud*, ed. Ernst Freud (London: Hogarth Press; 1961), p. 215.

3. "Contributions to a Discussion on Masturbation," *Standard Edition*, Vol. 12, p. 250.

4. Interview with Mrs. Alexander Freud, May 12, 1966.

5. *Letters*, pp. 58, 66.

6. *The Origins of Psychoanalysis*, ed. Marie Bonaparte (London: Imago; 1954), p. 227.

7. Jones: *Life of Freud*, III, 99.

8. Ibid., II, 386.

9. "Leonardo da Vinci," *Standard Edition*, Vol. 11, p. 101.

10. Interviews with Dr. Esti Freud, April 30, 1966, and August 27, 1966.

11. *Minutes*, II, 413.

12. Interviews with Dr. Esti Freud.

13. Interview with Oliver Freud.

14. Interview with Dr. Molly Putnam, September 22, 1966.

15. Interviews with Dr. Esti Freud.

16. Quoted in Jones: *Life of Freud*, III, 213.

17. "On Narcissism," *Standard Edition*, Vol. 14, p. 89. Cf. also letter of Max Schur to Jones, September 30, 1955 (Jones Archives).

18. Andreas-Salomé: *The Freud Journal*, p. 44.

19. Ibid., p. 57.

20. *Minutes*, II, p. 467.

21. Wittels: *Sigmund Freud*, p. 134.

22. The paper was Robert Waelder's, published as "Review of Freud's *Hemmung, Symptom und Angst*," *International Journal of Psychoanalysis*, X (1929), 103–11.

23. Andreas-Salomé: *The Freud Journal*, pp. 38–9.

24. Ibid., p. 169.

25. Ibid., pp. 51, 56.

26. Binion: *Frau Lou*, p. 401.

27. Andreas-Salomé: *The Freud Journal*, p. 57.

28. Ibid., pp. 57–8.

29. Wittels: *Sigmund Freud*, p. 150.

30. Hanns Sachs: *Freud, Master and Friend* (London: Imago; 1945), p. 69.

31. "An Autobiographical Study," *Standard Edition*, Vol. 20, p. 11.

32. *Letters*, pp. 313–14.

33. Andreas-Salomé: *The Freud Journal*, p. 97.

34. Ibid., p. 114.

35. Ibid., p. 97.

36. Ibid., p. 98.

37. Ibid., p. 114.

38. Ibid., p. 88.

39. Ibid., pp. 166–7. The past tense in this last sentence does make one wonder whether she wrote it years later.

40. Ibid., p. 166.

41. Ibid., p. 167.

42. Ibid., pp. 167–8. The concept "beast of prey" comes from Freud's essay "On Narcissism." "The charm of a child lies to a great extent in his narcissism, his self-contentment and inaccessibility, just as does the charm of certain animals which seem not to concern themselves about us, such as cats and the large beasts of prey." Cf. "On Narcissism," *Standard Edition*, Vol. 14, p. 89.

Chapter III

1. "Zur Psychologie des Deserteurs," *Internationale Zeitschrift für Psychoanalyse*, Vol. 4 (1916), pp. 193–204, 229–40. Translations of these papers appear in *Psychoanalytic Quarterly*, Vol. 38 (1969).

2. Binion: *Frau Lou*, pp. 358–9.

3. "Recommendations to Physicians Practising Psychoanalysis," *Standard Edition*, Vol. 12, p. 116.

4. Nunberg: *Minutes*, I, xxii.

5. In an article on "Didactic Analysis," Hanns Sachs argued that "analysis needs something corresponding to the novitiate of the Church." *Ten Years of the Berlin Psychoanalytic Institute* (Vienna: International Psychoanalytic Association; 1930), p. 45.

6. Letter of Anna Freud to Jones, March 7, 1955 (Jones Archives).

7. Andreas-Salomé: *The Freud Journal*, p. 169.

8. Interview with Dr. Robert Jokl, December 28, 1965.

9. Interview with Dr. Herman Nunberg, April 1, 1967.

10. Dr. Richard Wagner speaks of his "personal secession" from

the Vienna Society for this reason. Interview, December 17, 1965.

11. Interview with Dr. Helene Deutsch, February 7, 1966.

12. Interview with Dr. Philip Sarasin, November 30, 1966.

13. Quoted in A. E. Hotchner: *Papa Hemingway* (New York: Bantam Books; 1967), p. 51.

14. "On the History of the Psychoanalytic Movement," *Standard Edition*, Vol. 14, p. 22.

15. "Recommendations to Physicians Practising Psychoanalysis," *Standard Edition*, Vol. 12, p. 118.

16. In a book review published not long after Tausk's death, Jones did brush Tausk off as "a paraphrenic who could come to no other end." "Paraphrenia" was for a while the term proposed by Freud instead of the more familiar schizophrenia or dementia praecox. "Book review of Wittel's *Freud*," *International Journal of Psychoanalysis*, Vol. 5, Part 4 (October 1924), pp. 481–6.

  Jones also told an associate that Tausk had "caught" schizophrenia. In the early 1920's psychoses were even more mysterious to psychoanalysts than today. So Jones could well have looked upon schizophrenia as an illness one might catch like a common cold. Interview with Professor L. S. Penrose, August 31, 1965.

17. Jones: *Life of Freud*, II, 429.

18. *The Letters of Sigmund Freud and Karl Abraham*, eds. Hilda Abraham and Ernst Freud (London: Hogarth Press; 1965), p. 345.

19. Quoted in Jessie Taft: *Otto Rank* (New York: Julian Press; 1958), p. 107.

20. Published in English as "Compensation as a Means of Discounting the Motive of Repression," *International Journal of Psychoanalysis*, Vol. 5 (1924), pp. 130–40.

21. Interview with Dr. Edoardo Weiss, April 5, 1965.

22. "An Autobiographical Study," *Standard Edition*, Vol. 20, pp. 14–15.

23. Albert Hirst's letter to Ernest Jones, November 6, 1953, and to Anna Freud, October 19, 1953. Also Jones's letter to Albert Hirst, November 10, 1953 (Jones Archives).

24. July 23, 1904, and July 26, 1904. Cf. Richard Pfennig: *Wilhelm Fliess* (Berlin: Goldschmidt; 1906), pp. 26–9. Ernest Jones complained of Freud's indiscretion about one of Jones's ideas to a patient, Jekels, who then scooped Jones by writing it up himself. Cf. Jones: *Life of Freud*, III, 191.

25. July 27, 1904. Pfennig: *Wilhelm Fliess*, pp. 30–1.

26. Cf. Bernfeld's letter to Jones, May 26, 1952 (Jones Archives). Cf. Freud's letter to Karl Kraus, *Letters*, pp. 259–60.

27. *Minutes*, II, 48–9.

28. "Introductory Lectures," *Standard Edition*, Vol. 16, p. 257.

29. E. A. Bennet: "The Freud-Janet Controversy," *British Medical Journal*, January 2, 1965, pp. 52–3.

30. Quoted in David Shakow and David Rapaport: *The Influence of Freud on American Psychology* (New York: International Universities Press, 1964), p. 118.

31. "Introductory Lectures," Vol. 16, p. 285. "A Difficulty in the Path of Psychoanalysis," *Standard Edition*, Vol. 17, pp. 139–41.

32. Quoted in Jones: *Life of Freud*, III, 131.

33. Interview with Dr. Helene Deutsch, June 11, 1966.

34. "Analysis Terminable and Interminable," *Standard Edition*, Vol. 23, pp. 244–5.

35. Quoted in Ernst Kris: "Freud in the History of Science," *The Listener*, Vol. 55 (May 17, 1956), p. 631. Cf. my *Freud: Political and Social Thought*, pp. 84–5, for other reasons Freud had for not reading Nietzsche.

Chapter IV

1. Interviews with Professor Mark Brunswick, January 25, 1966, November 22, 1967, and Dr. Philip Sarasin.

2. I am indebted to Dr. Alan Tyson for this point.

3. "The Psychopathology of Everyday Life," *Standard Edition*, Vol. 6, p. 156.

4. "New Introductory Lectures," *Standard Edition*, Vol. 22, p. 134. "Civilized Sexual Morality and Modern Nervousness," *Standard Edition*, Vol. 9, pp. 195, 199. "Some Psychical Consequences of the Anatomical Distinctions Between the Sexes," *Standard Edition*, Vol. 19, p. 257.

5. "Civilization and Its Discontents," *Standard Edition*, Vol. 21, p. 103.

6. Siegfried Bernfeld: "On Psychoanalytic Training," *The Psychoanalytic Quarterly*, Vol. 31, No. 4 (1962), p. 463.

7. "A Short Account of Psychoanalysis," *Standard Edition*, Vol. 19, p. 203.

8. According to Kata Levy, her own analysis with Freud began at the time of the Budapest Congress, and Anna was already in analysis with her father then. When Oliver Freud visited home in 1921 his sister Anna was then in analysis with their father. Mrs. Edward Hitschmann, Dr. Anny Katan, Dr. Edith Jackson, Dr. Herman Nunberg, Dr. Irmarita Putnam, and Dr. Sandor Rado have all confirmed that Freud did indeed analyze Anna.

9. Binswanger: *Sigmund Freud*, p. 67.

10. Jones: *Life of Freud*, III, 4.

11. Ibid., p. 50.

12. For professional reasons she appeared on the stage as Hilde "Loewe."

13. Dr. H. W. Frink of New York.

14. *Minutes*, II, 335.

15. "Dreams and Telepathy," *Standard Edition*, Vol. 18, p. 197.

16. "An Autobiographical Study," *Standard Edition*, Vol. 20, p. 53.

17. Binswanger: *Sigmund Freud*, p. 9.

18. Franz Kafka: "Letter to His Father," in *Dearest Father* (New York: Schocken Books; 1954), p. 190, p. 188.

19. "New Introductory Lectures," *Standard Edition*, Vol. 22, p. 133.

20. Quoted in Jones: *Life of Freud*, III, 20.

21. "Some Neurotic Mechanisms in Jealousy, Paranoia and Homosexuality," *Standard Edition*, Vol. 18, p. 228.

22. Kafka: "Letter to His Father," p. 196.

Chapter V

1. Kurt Eissler: *Medical Orthodoxy and the Future of Psychoanalysis* (New York: International Universities Press; 1965), p. 237.

2. A maxim of Sadger's. Cf. *On Suicide*, ed. Paul Friedman (New York: International Universities Press; 1967), p. 22.

3. Quoted in ibid.

4. "The Psychogenesis of a Case of Homosexuality in a Woman," *Standard Edition*, Vol. 18, p. 162.

5. Peter Sifneos: "Manipulative Suicide," *The Psychiatric Quarterly* (July 1966), p. 4 (reprint).

6. Karl Menninger: "Discussion," *International Journal of Psychiatry*, Vol. 2, No. 2 (March 1966), p. 196.

7. Edwin Stengel: "Enquiries into Attempted Suicide," *Proceedings of the Royal Society of Medicine*, Vol. 45 (1952), p. 618.

8. "Victor Tausk," *Standard Edition*, Vol. 17, pp. 273–5.

9. *Psychoanalysis and Faith*, ed. Heinrich Meng and Ernst Freud (New York: Basic Books; 1963), p. 71.

10. Sigmund Freud–Lou Andreas-Salomé: *Briefwechsel* (Frankfurt: Fischer; 1966), p. 108. For a slightly different but unexpurgated translation of this letter, cf. Binion: *Frau Lou*, p. 402–3.

11. *Letters*, pp. 73–80.

12. "My Contact with Josef Popper-Lynkeus," *Standard Edition*, Vol. 22, p. 224.

13. By September 1919 Freud sent a manuscript of *Beyond the Pleasure Principle*, begun in March, to friends.

14. Binion: *Frau Lou*, p. 403.

15. Ruth Mack Brunswick: "A Supplement to Freud's 'History of an Infantile Neurosis,'" in *The Psychoanalytic Reader*, ed. Robert Fleiss (New York: International Universities Press; 1948), p. 103.

16. Freud later admitted that he had been at first reluctant to analyze the negative reactions of his patients. Cf. "Analysis Terminable and Interminable," *Standard Edition*, Vol. 23, pp. 221–2.

17. Ibid., p. 249.

18. "Introductory Lectures on Psychoanalysis," *Standard Edition*, Vol. 16, p. 463.

19. *Minutes*, II, 29.

20. Weiss: *Structure and Dynamics of the Human Mind*, p. xviii.

21. Interviews with Dr. Robert Jokl.

22. Quoted in Jones: *Life of Freud*, II, 415.

23. *Letters*, pp. 295–6.

24. Andreas-Salomé: *The Freud Journal*, p. 163.

Chapter VI

1. Cf. Kurt Eissler's interview with Paul Klemperer (Jones Archives).

2. Letter from Freud to J. J. Putnam, August 20, 1912 (Jones Archives).

3. Interviews with Richard Wagner, December 17, 1965, February 11, 1966, and March 25, 1966.

4. "An Autobiographical Study," *Standard Edition*, Vol. 20, p. 53.

5. "On the History of the Psychoanalytic Movement," *Standard Edition*, Vol. 14, p. 51.

6. Ibid. For a similar problem between Freud and Groddeck, cf. *Letters*, pp. 322–4.

7. Quoted in Andreas-Salomé: *The Freud Journal*, p. 161.
8. Wittels: *Sigmund Freud*, p. 138.
9. Edith V. Weigert: "Dissent in the Early History of Psychoanalysis," *Psychiatry*, Vol. 5 (1942), p. 354.
10. *Letters*, p. 265.
11. For Freud's relation to Jung, cf. my *Freud: Political and Social Thought*, pp. 23–5, 126, 135–6, 156, 161–2, 169, 178–80, 189, and 224–5.
12. Jones: *Life of Freud*, I, 317.
13. Interview with Dr. Edward Bennet, November 9, 1966.
14. *Letters*, p. 304.
15. Binswanger: *Sigmund Freud*, p. 53.
16. "New Introductory Lectures on Psychoanalysis," *Standard Edition*, Vol. 22, pp. 143–4.
17. "On the History of the Psychoanalytic Movement," ibid., Vol. 14, p. 7.
18. Sachs: *Freud, Master and Friend*, pp. 95–6.
19. *Letters of Freud and Abraham*, p. 141.
20. Sachs: *Freud, Master and Friend*, p. 114.
21. *Letters*, p. 339.
22. "Psychoanalysis and Telepathy," *Standard Edition*, Vol. 18, p. 178.
23. Quoted in Jones: *Life of Freud*, III, 395.
24. Andreas-Salomé: *The Freud Journal*, p. 169.
25. Quoted in Jones: *Life of Freud*, III, 391.
26. Ibid., II, 14.
27. "Psychopathology of Everyday Life," *Standard Edition*, Vol. 6, p. 256.
28. Ibid., p. 260.
29. Ibid.
30. "Introductory Lectures," *Standard Edition*, Vol. 16, p. 438.
31. "New Introductory Lectures," *Standard Edition*, Vol. 22, p. 159.
32. "Beyond the Pleasure Principle," *Standard Edition*, Vol. 18, p. 59.
33. Paul Schilder: "The Influence of Psychoanalysis on Psychiatry,"

The Psychoanalytic Quarterly, Vol. 9, No. 2 (1940), pp. 216–17.

34. Ibid., p. 220.

35. "On Psychotherapy," *Standard Edition*, Vol. 7, p. 263.

36. "A Short Account of Psychoanalysis," *Standard Edition*, Vol. 19, p. 204.

37. "Analysis Terminable and Interminable," *Standard Edition*, Vol. 23, p. 235.

38. "The Claims of Psychoanalysis to Scientific Interest," *Standard Edition*, Vol. 13, p. 174, and "Introductory Lectures," Vol. 16, p. 415.

39. "Freud's Psychoanalytic Procedure," *Standard Edition*, Vol. 7, p. 250.

40. "An Autobiographical Study," *Standard Edition*, Vol. 20, p. 60.

41. Binswanger: *Sigmund Freud*, p. 37.

42. Andreas-Salomé: *The Freud Journal*, p. 72.

43. "Freud as a Psychoanalytic Consultant—Letters to Edoardo Weiss," ed. Martin Grotjahn, *The Psychoanalytic Forum*, Vol. 1, No. 1 (1966), pp. 136–7. Ruth Mack Brunswick, who saw Freud's "Wolfman" in treatment, suggested that Freud's cure of some neurotic defenses may have opened the way to the expression of far more primitive mechanisms. "A Supplement to Freud's 'History of an Infantile Neurosis,'" in *The Psychoanalytic Reader*, p. 101.

44. Edoardo Weiss: *Agoraphobia in the Light of Ego Psychology* (New York: Grune & Stratton; 1964), p. 6.

45. When Hollos and Federn went to Freud with a book on psychotics edited by Meng, Freud said "These people are uncanny" as he put it aside. Interview with Ernst Federn, June 24, 1966.

46. "Freud Correspondence," *The Psychoanalytic Quarterly*, Vol. 25 (1956), p. 361.

47. *Letters*, p. 390.

48. S. Freud: *Psychoanalysis and Faith*, p. 61.

49. Quoted in Jones: *Life of Freud*, II, 417–18.

50. "An Autobiographical Study," *Standard Edition*, Vol. 20, p. 8;

"The Question of Lay Analysis," *Standard Edition*, Vol. 20, p. 254; and *Letters*, p. 241.

51. "Freud as a Psychoanalytic Consultant," p. 135.

52. "Two Encyclopaedia Articles," *Standard Edition*, Vol. 18, p. 250.

53. Interview with Elma Laurvik, April 3, 1967.

54. *Letters*, p. 287.

55. Andreas-Salomé: *The Freud Journal*, p. 83.

56. Edoardo Weiss: "My Acquaintanceship with Victor Tausk" (unpublished manuscript), p. 3.

57. "Sigmund Freud as a Consultant and Therapist: From Freud's Letters to Edoardo Weiss," ed. Martin Grotjahn, *The Psychoanalytic Forum*, Vol. 1, No. 2 (1966), p. 228. And "Freud as a Psychoanalytic Consultant," pp. 134–5.

58. Wortis: *Fragment of an Analysis with Freud*, p. 80.

59. "Five Lectures on Psychoanalysis," *Standard Edition*, Vol. 11, p. 53.

60. Cf. Bertram Lewin's obituary of Federn, *The Psychoanalytic Quarterly*, Vol. 19 (1950), p. 296.

According to Weiss, Federn never acknowledged publicly Tausk's priority for the concept of ego boundaries, and this stemmed from Federn's anger at Tausk's advances to his wife Wilma.

61. Cf. Edoardo Weiss: "Federn's Concepts and Their Applicability to the Understanding and Treatment of Schizophrenia," *The Journal of Nervous and Mental Disease*, Vol. 133, No. 2 (August 1961), pp. 155–60.

62. Erik Erikson: *Identity: Youth and Crisis* (New York: Norton; 1968), p. 9.

63. Edith Jacobson: *The Self and the Object World* (New York: International Universities Press; 1964), p. xi.

64. Weiss: *The Structure and Dynamics of the Human Mind*, p. xiv.

65. *Minutes*, II, 388.

Notes

66. Ibid., pp. 297, 379.
67. "Lines of Advance in Psychoanalytic Therapy," *Standard Edition*, Vol. 17, p. 165.
68. Tausk: "Diagnostic Consideration Regarding the Symptomatology of the So-Called War Psychoses," *The Psychoanalytic Quarterly*, Vol. 38 (1969).
69. Ibid.
70. Wittels: *Sigmund Freud*, pp. 130–1.
71. Jones: *Life of Freud*, II, 411–12.
72. Tausk: "On the Origin of the 'Influencing Machine' in Schizophrenia," in *The Psychoanalytic Reader*, p. 64. Hanns Sachs developed this notion in his "Delay of the Machine Age," *The Psychoanalytic Quarterly*, Vol. 2 (1933), pp. 404–24.
73. "The Unconscious," *Standard Edition*, Vol. 14, p. 197.
74. Cf. Gordon Globus and Richard Pillard: "Tausk's 'Influencing Machine' and Kafka's 'In the Penal Colony,'" *American Imago*, Vol. 23, No. 3 (Fall 1966), pp. 191–207.
75. Bruno Bettelheim: "Joey: A 'Mechanical Boy,'" in *Frontiers of Psychological Research*, ed. Stanley Coopersmith (San Francisco: W. H. Freeman; 1966), pp. 222–9. Cf. also Bettelheim: *The Empty Fortress* (New York: The Free Press; 1967), pp. 233–339. Cf. also Bettelheim: *The Informed Heart* (Glencoe: The Free Press; 1960), p. 58.

Afterward

1. Tausk: "Ibsen, The Druggist," *Psychoanalytic Quarterly*, Vol. 3 (1934), p. 141.

ACKNOWLEDGMENTS

My wife, Deborah Heller Roazen, has lovingly edited this book for me. I would also like to thank, for financial assistance, the Canady Humanities Fund of Harvard College, the Social Science Research Council Faculty Grants Committee, and the Foundation's Fund for Research in Psychiatry.

INDEX

VINTAGE WORKS OF SCIENCE
AND PSYCHOLOGY

VINTAGE CRITICISM,
LITERATURE, MUSIC, AND ART